FINANCIAL DIMENSIONS OF MARKETING MANAGEMENT

SERIES ON MARKETING MANAGEMENT

Series Editor: **FREDERICK E. WEBSTER, Jr.**
*The Amos Tuck School
of Business Administration
Dartmouth College*

GEORGE S. DOMINGUEZ, *Marketing in a Regulated Environment*
ROBERT D. ROSS, *The Management of Public Relations: Analysis and
Planning External Relations*
VICTOR WADEMAN, *Risk-Free Advertising: How to Come
Close to It*
FRANK H. MOSSMAN, W. J. E. CRISSY, and PAUL M. FISCHER,
Financial Dimensions of Marketing Management

Financial Dimensions
of Marketing Management

FRANK H. MOSSMAN

**Michigan State University
East Lansing, Michigan**

W. J. E. CRISSY

**Michigan State University
East Lansing, Michigan**

PAUL M. FISCHER

**University of Wisconsin-Milwaukee
Milwaukee, Wisconsin**

A Ronald Press PUBLICATION

JOHN WILEY & SONS
New York • Chichester • Brisbane • Toronto

Library of Congress Cataloging in Publication Data:

Mossman, Frank Homer.
    Financial dimensions of marketing management.

    Series on marketing management
    "A Ronald Press publication."
    Includes indexes.
    1. Marketing management—Finance. I. Crissy, William Joseph Eliot,
joint author. II. Fischer, Paul M., joint author. III. Title.

HF5415.13.M68   658.1'55   77-14990
ISBN 0-471-03376-6

Printed in the United States of America

10 9 8 7 6 5 4 3 2 1

SERIES EDITOR'S FOREWORD

Marketing management is among the most dynamic of the business functions. On the one hand it reflects the everchanging marketplace and the constant evolution of customer preferences and buying habits, and of competition. On the other hand, it grows continually in sophistication and complexity as developments in management science are applied to the work of the marketing manager. If he or she is to be a true management professional, the marketing person must stay informed about these developments.

The Wiley Series on Marketing Management has been developed to serve this need. The books in the series have been written for managers. They combine a concern for management application with an appreciation for the relevance of developments in such areas of management science as behavioral science, financial analysis, and mathematical modeling, as well as the insights gained from analyzing successful experience in the market place. The Wiley Series on Marketing Management is thus intended to communicate the state-of-the-art in marketing to managers.

Virtually all areas of marketing management will be explored in the series. Books now available or being planned cover advertising management, industrial marketing research, brand loyalty, sales management, product policy and planning, public relations, overall marketing strategy, and financial aspects of marketing management. It is hoped that the

series will have some effect in raising the standards of applied marketing
management.

FREDERICK E. WEBSTER, JR.

Hanover, New Hampshire
June, 1977

Foreword

The writers have provided a useful source of information for all managers concerned with profitability—and that is just about everybody. Financial and marketing executives will view the book as a valuable guide in refining policies and procedures to aid in the identification of profitable opportunities.

The main objective of this book is to show how the financial data-gathering system can assimilate comprehensive data on the appropriate disaggregated basis for defined market segments. To this end, a highly desirable feature of the book is that each concept is reinforced with one or more examples.

Commendably, the writers also discuss the spectrum of information beyond the financial data needed for market planning and decision making. Thus cost/revenue/profit data are put in a realistic perspective.

Implicit in the presentation is the need for close communication and coordination between financial and marketing executives. The successful implementation of segmental analysis is a joint endeavor.

The system espoused provides for timely information, direct costing, and segmental budgeting. Executives who adopt the writers' proposals must ensure that their people understand and appreciate the benefits to the firm and to them individually. This approach could add a key dimension to appraisal of performance, namely, profit contribution.

ARCHIE M. LONG
Comptroller
General Motors Corporation
Detroit, Michigan

Preface

Financial Dimensions of Marketing has grown out of the individual and joint consulting experiences of the writers. The initial stimulus for the book may have been the participation of Fischer and Mossman in the American Accounting Association project on marketing profit analysis in 1972.

Hopefully, the book will be viewed as a guide for those concerned with improving the financial performance of the marketing effort. It is not a conventional text, though some instructors may use it as a supplementary source of information in courses concerned with cost/revenue/profit analysis.

We have chosen to limit detailed coverage to those topics that comprise a framework for understanding and applying segmental analysis and profit contribution to the firm. The illustrative materials are "real-world" applications. Their diversity shows that firms of all sizes in both the consumer and industrial sector can use the principles and methods as set forth.

It is our intent to continue research and practice in this field and consequently we shall be very grateful for comments, criticisms, and additional illustrations.

FRANK H. MOSSMAN
W. J. E. CRISSY
PAUL M. FISCHER

East Lansing, Michigan
Milwaukee, Wisconsin
August, 1977

Contents

ONE

Introduction, 1

The case is established for the development of precise cost/revenue/profit data on a real-time basis. It is assumed that financial responsibility will be decentralized; thus, detailed, disaggregated information is imperative. Past attempts to analyze the profitability of marketing efforts have taken the form of special statistical studies imposed over existing aggregated accounting data. These methods provide only indicators and do not provide a continuing integrated information system for marketing decision-making. The approach used in this book is based on *contribution theory* rather than *full-cost allocation*. A modular data base is advocated which provides the data necessary to both minimize the cost of promotion, production, and physical distribution and to measure the financial performance of a broad variety of marketing segments. Contribution theory as made operational by the suggested data base is used to present various financial tools which may be used to maximize the profitability of marketing efforts.

TWO

Accounting for Marketing Segments, 7

Contribution theory is applied as segments are viewed as a gathering place for all revenues they produce and costs which they specifically require.

Costs are separated according to their behavior with respect to volume and their controllability with respect to time frames and management discretion. This allows the financial impact of a segment to be measured on a short- and long-run basis at alternative sales levels. Investment in assets necessitated by a segment can be considered using the return on investment type model; however, a residual income approach is advocated as being a better tool. This approach actually levies an "interest" cost for assets used by a segment.

THREE

An Operational System for Contribution Analysis, 25

A modular data base systems design is presented to make contribution analysis operational. The system uses a common data base to measure the performance of functional costs of production and physical distribution, to measure the contribution of marketing segments, and to prepare external statements. The chapter includes an analysis of the demands that may be placed on the system so that they may be considered in its design.

FOUR

Forecasting and Monitoring Markets, 52

Revenues, costs, and technology forecasting are related to short-term, intermediate, and long-term marketing plans. Both the deductive approach, which starts with aggregate measures applied down to segments, and the inductive approach, which begins with forecasts at the field sales level, are analyzed. The deductive and inductive approaches are then reflected in a summary of the customer-product mix and compared to the product-service levels, both by segment and aggregatively for the firm.

FIVE

Developing a Marketing Information System, 69

The very amount and diversity of marketing information points up the need to formalize a marketing information system (MIS) for the firm. Criteria are presented for the establishment of such a system followed by a discussion of the principal kinds and sources of marketing information. An operational model is suggested to facilitate the establishment of an MIS system. Criteria of effectiveness serve to judge the success of the system.

SIX

Programming the Firm's Competitive Effort, 81

An evaluation is made of the general considerations that determine the stage of a life cycle of a segment. This evaluation is necessary in order to optimally plan and program the firm's competitive effort and to convert these competitive plans into financial requirements. Specific consideration is given to the financial requirements at each stage of the life cycle. These are interrelated with the programming of the firm's promotional effort at the segmental and aggregative levels.

SEVEN

Programming the Physical Distribution Function, 101

The uniqueness of physical distribution costs is compared to other functional costs from the following points of view: the need for costs of external suppliers (intercity carriers, warehousing, etc.) to be blended with internal costs, the nature of increasing unit cost as geographic dispersion of the market increases, the effects on customers from external-imposed conditions, and the problems posed by geographic dispersion of inventories. The theory and practice of trade-offs is considered at three levels: within the subfunctions, between the subfunctions, and the effect of the trade-off on the revenue of the segments.

EIGHT

Budgeting for Operational Planning and Control, 120

Criteria are presented for developing a marketing budget together with the steps used in budget preparation. The budget is viewed as a planning and control device incorporating product and customer-related attachable variable and fixed costs as well as revenues. The basic analysis consists of the hierarchy of segment analysis, information requirements, an example of model application, and the analysis of a marketing plan. Optimization of segment contributions and variance analysis are presented as management tools.

NINE

Strategic and Tactical Implementation, 136

Successful implementation of the concepts embodied in the contribution approach require an effective understanding of the responsibilities of both the financial and marketing executives. It must also be understood that the performance of a segment as an analytic unit is usually not the direct responsibility of any one manager but rather reflects the interaction of many members of the management team. Emerging developments in marketing efficiency are studied. Issues in salesmen's motivation and incremental performance measures are explained. It is also suggested that nonfinancial productivity measures be utilized to supplement financial measures.

Tables

Figures

FINANCIAL DIMENSIONS
OF MARKETING MANAGEMENT

CHAPTER 1

Introduction

⌈To stay competitive in a rapidly changing business world, companies must have the information they need to determine quickly the actual and potentially profitable and unprofitable segments[1] of their business.⌉ This means that there must be an increased emphasis on the ability to react to changing markets regardless of whether the reason for change comes from sources internal or external to the business. Management must be capable of planning alternative courses of action and must be able to determine what these alternative courses will do to the profit picture of the company.⌉

Tunnel vision and myopia must be avoided. A narrow outlook may lead to missed market opportunities and, at a minimum, a loss of timely information concerning competitive activity. Myopia may result in management by expediency and prevent intermediate and long-term benefits being realized. Computers have made possible the ready availability of timely information for all segments of a firm which reflects the interrelationships of accounting and marketing information. Costs and revenues may be quickly attached to segments and functional centers.[2]

HISTORICAL PERSPECTIVE

The interrelationship between accounting and marketing has not been well developed in the past. In order to understand the nature of the

[1] By "segments" we mean market groupings with common needs and wants, individual products and product groups, shipments, and geographic sectors ranging from sales territories to foreign nations.

[2] By "functional centers" we mean such suborganizations as sales, advertising, inventory control, and warehousing.

1

problem it is necessary to understand the historical role of accounting and the information that it has provided to the business. It is also important to consider how modern marketing management has evolved.

In its historical role the balance sheet was developed originally to provide investors and lending institutions information on the assets of the firm and the amount of ownership equity in the business. The balance sheet is a statement of assets, equities, and liabilities at a particular point in time. However, per se it provides little information of value concerning the profit performance of a firm; that is not its intent.

As businesses developed greater sophistication it became necessary to provide information to lending institutions on what happened in the business enterprise between balance sheet dates, and to do this the income statement evolved. The profit-and-loss statement is an aggregate statement of revenues and expenses between two specified dates. Due to the aggregated nature of the information, neither the balance sheet nor the income statement provide much usable information to marketing management.

In order to provide an amalgam of this information, a whole spectrum of asset and equity accounts (balance sheet) and income and expense accounts (income statement) was developed. These came to be known as the natural accounts as indicated in Figure 1.1.

This process is basically aggregative. For example, the basic documents for hourly rated labor are time slips. These are aggregated into a natural account which might be called factory labor. These natural accounts are further aggregated into the balance sheet asset and equity accounts and the revenue and expense accounts. These aggregative processes basically meet the *external* accounting needs of the business and comprise traditional accounting.

Until recently the focus in marketing has been on generating sales, and the key yardstick of effectiveness has been growth in revenue. While lip service was given to profit, financial data needed to define and measure profit were lacking. Marketing management had little communication with accounting. Only rarely did detailed cost-revenue analysis occur. People in marketing and especially in sales tended to view the

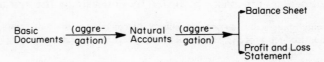

Figure 1.1.   Aggregation of costs.

financial staff with suspicion, perhaps as a defense mechanism for their own fiscal naîveté. Wide profit margins, characteristic of the post-World War II economy, hid many management sins.

More recently, as natural resources became depleted, the energy crisis occurred, and a general slowdown in economic growth resulted. Business commenced to focus on profit and, in marketing, this means *selectivity*. Firms withdrew from marginal markets and narrowed their product service offerings. These interrelated phenomena pointed up the need for accounting concepts and tools which would enable marketing management to gain a precise cost/revenue/profit picture.

Development of Information for Internal Analysis

The traditional aggregative process, appropriate to external needs, severely limits the use of the natural accounts for needed internal diagnosis and analysis. Therefore, some development had to evolve to meet the needs for internal analysis, and this is illustrated in Figure 1.2.

In this process the natural accounts are disaggregated into *functional* cost centers and thence reaggregated into segmental cost centers for analytical purposes. The functional cost centers—such as production, warehousing, storage, and marketing—are the principal activity centers of the business; other functional and subfunctional centers may be established for the control of the business operation. The need for detailed functional cost information is apparent to assure the efficient operation of each of the functional parts of the business. It is mandatory for effective marketing planning and control. After all, marketing consists of a selective search for targets and the mobilization of resources to capitalize on them once they are defined.

This disaggregative process starts with the natural accounts, and disaggregates them into centers that will be useful for functional cost planning and control. As an illustration of this procedure, the costs of a motor carrier can be disaggregated into the functional cost centers of terminal pickup costs, terminal delivery costs, terminal dock costs, and line haul costs between terminals. Means are developed for disaggregating the various natural accounts into each of these particular cost centers on a judgmental basis. The process is usually based on historical

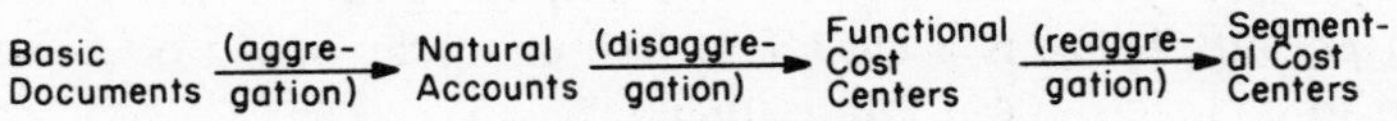

| Basic Documents | (aggregation) → | Natural Accounts | (disaggregation) → | Functional Cost Centers | (reaggregation) → | Segmental Cost Centers |

Figure 1.2.   Disaggregation of costs.

cost data aggregated into the natural accounts and then attached to the functional cost centers after the period in which the cost has been incurred. Functional cost accounting information is furnished to the functional manager and provides him with some basis for planning and control.

The traditional accounting process may be carried one step beyond functional costs—namely, to the determination of *segmental* costs. It is also possible under the traditional disaggregative process to distribute the costs as determined for the functional cost centers to the marketing segments which consume the services.

Each market segment may be viewed as an analytic unit where the results of each function's activity come together to produce a sale. For example, in the sale of products, the functions of warehousing, inventory, selling, advertising, and a host of other marketing and physical distribution functions are utilized to sell and deliver the product in the company's marketing effort. Therefore, one can conceive of the segment as consisting of the relevant functonal costs, and it is logical to combine these functional costs on a segmental basis in order to determine the cost of doing business by segments. Segment managers need this information in order to have some idea of what comparative costs are among different segments of the market.

Pretransactional Marketing Problems

In the pretransactional or promotional phase of marketing, special problems must be handled if costs and revenues are to be identified with specific efforts. First, if the total promotional program is properly designed it is difficult to isolate the impact of specific forces—for example, the relative effect of advertising, selling, sales promotion, and merchandising. They are synergistic! Each one enhances, reinforces, and interacts with the others. Second, often economies of scale dictate using specific forces to promote simultaneously more than one product and to cultivate more than one market. A commercial on national TV would be aimed at many market segments and might promote a company's entire product line. Consider the difficulty of isolating the effect of such an ad or even an entire advertising campaign on the movement of one product in the line or on demand in one market segment. Third, often the promotional impact is not fully realized in the current period. There is a lag effect. An example would be a concerted attempt to change the corporate image.

Transactional Marketing Problems

The transactional phase of marketing also presents some cost/revenue attachment problems. For instance, in many companies personal selling is a team operation. The salesman often must call upon supportive personnel such as engineering or finance to augment his efforts before a sale is made. Also, not infrequently a sale transcends the territory where it was consummated. Many firms centralize their purchasing. Kindred to this in difficulty is the situation where selling is done on a bid basis or by annual contract. The proposal may involve the efforts of many people transcending departmental lines. Still another complication is that in some businesses orders are phoned in or mailed—the field salesman himself is mainly a missionary. Thus in many situations it is not easy to answer the question: *What did this sale cost?*

Posttransactional Marketing Problems

It is probably in the posttransactional stage of marketing that the state of the art permits the most accurate cost analysis. That is why in later chapters we present applications of segmental analysis to physical distribution. Even here sticky problems arise. These include: order processing costs by customer and by product; internal materials handling and other costs associated with order filling; transportation and delivery costs. Economies of scale often require automation as well as the combination of products and orders. Yet these very savings often prevent isolation and attachment of costs to account, to product, or to order.

IMPLEMENTATION OF THE CONTRIBUTION APPROACH

Basic theory for analyzing the financial performance of marketing segments is developed in Chapter 2. The traditional net income approach, which fully allocates all costs to a segment, is replaced by a more modern approach which attaches to a segment only those costs incurred specifically for the segment. The behavior of costs according to volume, time frames, and management discretion are considered from both the short- and long-run points of view. Consideration is given to segmental investments in assets by comparing return on investment and the residual income approach in which "interest" costs for assets used by a segment are charged to the segment.

An operational system for cost and revenue flows is presented in Chapter 3. The use of a modular data base is suggested that will allow prompt retrieval of the cost and revenue information by both the segmental managers and functional cost center managers for purposes of planning and control.

A major part of the planning effort of both the segment managers and functional center managers is a knowledge of the future efforts required both at the company level and at the market segment level. The subject of forecasting and monitoring markets is presented in Chapter 4. A matrix approach is used to present the inductive forecast of demand estimates at the market segment levels. The deductive approach starts with aggregate measures, and proceeds deductively to the segmental level. These two approaches are combined in a summary of the customer-product mix and compared to the product service levels in the various market segments.

Closely aligned to the forecasting and monitoring of markets is the need for the development of a market information system. An operational model for a system to facilitate needed information flow for the contribution approach is suggested in Chapter 5.

Implementation of the contribution concept requires programming by managers at both the segmental and functional levels. Optimal planning and programming of the firm's competitive efforts and conversion of these competitive plans into financial requirements are considered in Chapter 6. Planning and programming of physical distribution costs are considered in Chapter 7. The physical distribution function is considered in detail because of its close interrelationship to functional marketing costs.

Translation into financial terms of the firm's plans for future activities is presented in the budget for operational planning and control in Chapter 8. Criteria are presented for developing a marketing budget as a planning and control device utilizing the contribution approach. Optimization of segment contributions and variance analysis are considered as part of the planning and control tools of management.

Successful implementation of the contribution approach requires effective understanding and participation by both financial and marketing executives. The specific responsibilities of each one for implementation are considered in Chapter 9 together with a consideration of the more important emerging developments in financial dimensions of marketing profit analysis.

CHAPTER 2

Accounting

FOR

Market Segments

Marketing decisions should attune the performance of segments to maximize the profits of the firm. To facilitate this process, the accounting model must measure the contribution each existing segment makes to the total firm's common costs and profit. It must also estimate the contribution of proposed plans concerning existing or contemplated segments. The contribution of a segment will be termed "net segment margin," which is the excess of a segment's revenue over its attachable costs. Attachable costs are those that are incurred specifically for a segment and could be avoided if the segment were not to exist. No attempt is made to allocate common costs since they are seldom affected by any one segment's operations. For example, corporate headquarters' costs of a large corporation would not be in any way allocated to sales territories. This is not to say that the territories receive no benefits from such costs; rather, decisions made concerning the sales territory will have no material effect on corporate headquarters' costs, which are only attachable at that level.

The net segment margin model is an outgrowth of the accounting decision tool—incremental analysis. This tool holds that for any decision to be made only the costs and revenues affected should be compared. Inclusion of unaffected variables can only confound and confuse the analysis. As the net segment margin model for marketing decisions evolves, it must be made usable on both an estimated and actual basis. This flexibility will allow the model to be used for assessing alternatives

7

to arrive at a plan of operations and will also allow actual results to be meaningfully compared to the resulting plan.

DETERMINING COST BEHAVIOR

The usefulness of the model will be greatly enhanced if it is capable of estimating the performance of a market segment at alternative volume levels. For example, it may be desirable to compare the performance of two alternative products over a range of volumes rather than at single "most likely" volume levels. It is also desirable to know the "break-even" volume, which is the sales level at which a segment makes a zero contribution to corporate common costs. In essence, it is useful in assessing any alternative to measure the response of net segment margin with respect to volume over a relevant range of likely sales. To accomplish this analysis, a segment's costs must be separated into two basic groups:

1. Those that are incurred in a lump sum and will, once incurred, tend to be unaffected by volume over the anticipated range of sales. Such costs are often referred to as *fixed*. Note that fixed means "no observable relationship to volume" and not necessarily that the cost is not subject to management discretion. Rent, depreciation, and management salaries are examples of fixed costs.
2. Those that change in a predictable manner with respect to volume. Such costs are termed *variable*. Typically these costs are viewed as variable with sales volume. For example, many costs of manufacturing the product and distributing it vary on a one-to-one basis with unit volume. This relationship does not always hold; for example, the cost of a salesman's travel is a function of miles driven which may not in turn correlate with sales volume.

Table 2.1 is a simplified example of how net segment margin might be analyzed. Variable costs are deducted from revenue to produce a contribution margin of $360,000. Contribution margin is, in fact, the sales price of units sold reduced immediately for those costs that expire as each sale is made. The cumulative contribution margin of the units sold is then available to cover the specific "fixed costs" of the segment. The excess of the contribution margin over these fixed costs is termed the net segment margin. It is the amount available to cover the remaining common costs and profit of the firm. In summary, each unit sold contributed $3 (revenue of $8 minus variable production cost of $5)

TABLE 2.1   SIMPLE SEGMENTAL ANALYSIS

Revenue (120,000 units at $8 each)		$960,000
Less variable production cost (120,000 units at $5 each)		600,000
Segment contribution margin		360,000
Less specific fixed costs		
Salaries	$100,000	
Rent	50,000	
Utilities	5,000	155,000
Net segment margin		$205,000

to the fixed costs of the segment. In total the 120,000 units sold contributed $360,000 to cover the $155,000 of specific segment fixed costs. As a result the net segment margin of $205,000 is available to cover the remaining common costs and profit of the entire firm.

Graphically, Table 2.1 can be converted into the cost-profit-volume analysis shown in Figure 2.1. The specific cost function of the segment is shown to be $155,000 per period fixed cost plus $5 per unit variable cost. The revenue function is $8 per unit. The contribution of the segment at alternative volumes is found using the formula:

Net segment margin = Revenue − (Specific fixed costs +
variable cost per unit)

For 120,000 units:

Net segment margin = 120,000 × $8 − ($155,000 + $5 × 120,000)
= 960,000 − 755,000
= $205,000

The formula can also be solved to find the volume at which the segment just covers its own specific costs and makes zero contribution to the firm. This *break-even* volume is where the net segment margin is zero. Thus, using the above formula where X represents breakeven:

Net segment margin = Revenue − (Specific fixed costs +
Variable cost per unit)
$$0 = 8X − (\$155,000 + 5X)$$
$$0 = 8X − \$155,000 − 5X$$
$$3X = \$155,000$$
$$X = 51,667 \text{ units}$$

Obviously the break-even volume is always of secondary concern and

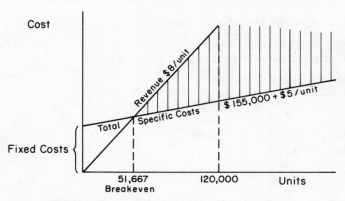

Figure 2.1.   Cost-profit-volume analysis.

merely aids assessment of the risk inherent in a segment. The risk might be quantified by stating how far below the forecast sales volume could fall before net segment margin becomes zero. For this example, sales could fall 68,333 units, or 57 percent. The real concern remains the response of net segment margin to volume.

Knowledge of cost behavior also aids control of segment costs since it allows the use of flexible budgeting. Flexible budgeting adjusts the level of allowable costs for changes in volume. This is in contrast to static budgeting which makes no provisions for alternative volume levels. For example, a static budget would, if used for the example of Table 2.1, state that the budgeted costs for the period to be $755,000 ($155,000 fixed cost plus $120,000 forecast units times the $5 variable unit cost). If the actual volume reached 130,000 units instead of the 120,000 planned units, no change would be made in budgeted costs. Thus, if $780,000 was spent by the segment to sell 130,000 units, the total deviation from the budget would be an overexpenditure of $25,000 ($780,000 actual less $755,000 budget). Flexible budgeting would, on the other hand, allow adjustment of budget for volume achieved. The budget would be stated as:

$155,000 per period plus $5 per unit.

Applying the budget to a volume of 130,000 units:

Budget = $155,000 + (130,000 units × $5 per unit)
         = $155,000 + $650,000
         = $805,000

Comparing the budget to the $780,000 actual expense indicates that

$25,000 less was spent than allowed. The full use of flexible budgeting for control of each segment will be discussed in Chapter 8.

COST BEHAVIOR PATTERNS

Production Costs

Most firms have accurate knowledge of the behavior of their production costs. Typically the direct labor and material costs are variable. Overhead tends to have both fixed and variable components. For example, machinery repair and power usage are typically variable, while depreciation of the plant and supervisory salaries are fixed. It should be noted that as increasing technology substitutes capital for labor, an increasing share of a firm's costs shift to fixed status. While actual production cost behavior is usually known and used by production management, it is often unavailable to marketing management. There are basically two reasons for this. First, the Internal Revenue Service and external accounting principles generally require that the per unit cost of an unsold product in the firm's inventory include a pro rata share of all production costs including variable and fixed elements. Thus, for product-costing purposes a full cost (variable cost plus a pro rata portion of fixed costs) has become common. Second, top management often feels that if the variable production cost of a unit were known it might be interpreted as a minimum acceptable sales price which, in time, might threaten the firm's ability to cover fixed costs. For these reasons marketing management may simply be told that a unit costs $15 to produce without being made aware that the variable cost is $12 and that $3 is tacked on to allow for the coverage of fixed costs. This blurring of cost behavior will confuse planning and cause faulty decisions. In the preceding example, the allocation of $3 per unit of fixed costs to each unit cannot be accepted since $3 per unit is of fixed cost and is not actually saved by not producing the unit.

Some firms defend full product costs by saying that fixed costs represent a charge for the use of capacity. A product not covering the charge should be dropped so that the capacity can be shifted to a product that can cover the charge. Such an argument would have merit, of course, only if the firm is operating at capacity. However, in Chapter 8 it will be argued that if a firm is at capacity, alternative uses of capacity must be specifically considered; an arbitrary charge for its use will not assure the correct decision.

Physical Distribution Costs

Physical distribution costs are typically treated with far less sophistication than production costs. Traditionally, this is due in part to the fact that physical distribution costs are not inventoried for tax or financial reporting purposes. Unlike production costs, which are incurred in advance of a sale and remain as assets in the inventory until sold, the majority of physical distribution costs are incurred at or subsequent to the time of sale. A second cause for the cursory consideration of physical distribution costs is that many separate types of functional costs make up the total set of physical distribution costs. Rather than isolate the cost behavior of each element, it has been convenient to merely view these costs as a part of fixed overhead.

Only lately, with the advent of the physical distribution system concept and the growth in physical distribution expenditures, has their behavior been scrutinized. Most firms will need physical distribution cost behavior knowledge to both plan their physical distribution costs and to charge for their usage by market segments. Analysis of physical distribution cost behavior is complicated by the multitude of factors that cause these costs to vary. While it would ease analysis if all physical distribution costs varied per unit of product sold, they often do not. Instead we find, for example, that transportation may vary by distance. This means that factors of cost variability other than units may be needed for these costs. As a result, a unique data collection system will be discussed in the section that follows. It will permit the attachment of physical distribution costs to segments by not only units sold but also such factors as number of invoices, number of invoice lines, miles shipped, and payment experience.

Promotion Costs

Promotion costs are typically fixed for a segment. That is, a level of expenditures is determined and sales flow is the anticipated result. Thus, the basic analytic procedure is to attach these costs in lump sums, unrelated to sales volume, to the segment for which they were specifically incurred. There may be some variable promotion costs such as sales commissions. Since these costs typically are a direct function of sales, they are easily attached to segments as a variable cost.

The attachability of variable costs to segments by factors of variability other than units complicates cost-profit-volume analysis. Any two-dimensional analysis of volume such as shown in Table 2.2 will by necessity require an assumed mix of product units and physical distribu-

TABLE 2.2   NET SEGMENT MARGIN

Revenue		$10,000,000	
Less variable costs			
Variable cost of goods sold (assumes a given product mix)	$5,400,000		(0.54 rev.)
Variable physical distribution costs (assumes given product & customer mix)	700,000		(0.07 rev.)
Variable sales commissions	300,000		(0.03 rev.)
Total variable costs		6,400,000	(0.64 rev.)
Segment contribution margin		3,600,000	(0.36 rev.)
Less short-run controllable fixed costs			
Fixed out-of-pocket service and distribution	600,000		
General and administrative	250,000		
Selling and advertising	150,000	1,000,000	
Segment Controllable Margin		2,600,000	
Less Long-Run Fixed Costs			
Depreciation on plant & equipment (based on change in market value)	350,000		
Lease expense, truck fleet	250,000	600,000	
Net segment margin		$2,000,000	

tion services. Sophisticated contribution analysis will require consideration of the behavior of the multiple factors of variability. Such analyses will be considered in Chapter 8.

CONSIDERING TIME FRAMES FOR FIXED COSTS

At some point in time all fixed costs attachable to a segment are subject to management's discretion. However, once a decision is made as to the level of some types of fixed costs they become a given for several future periods. For example, the purchase of a plant has the practical effect of committing a division to the plant in future years. A five-year lease of machinery tends to commit a division to the resulting rental in future periods. Such fixed costs are termed *long-run* committed costs. They are considered nondiscretionary for purposes of analysis during the period of commitment. Other fixed costs such as advertising or management salaries, which are discretionary during the period being analyzed, are considered *short-run* controllable costs.

Table 2.2 is an example of net segment margin analysis based on the above-mentioned differentiation of fixed costs. For the mix of products and physical distribution services implied, $.64 out of every sales dollar is spent for variable costs, and $.36 remains and is available to cover specific fixed costs. Some firms may wish to formally separate variable costs between production and nonproduction components. This may allow a comparison among segments of the relative magnitude of the various variable costs. Table 2.2 is often revised as follows in arriving at the segment contribution margin:

Revenue		$10,000,000
Less variable cost of goods sold		5,400,000
Gross variable margin		4,600,000
Less other variable costs:		
Physical distribution	$700,000	
Sales commissions	300,000	1,000,000
Segment Contribution Margin		$ 3,600,000

Continuing the analysis of Table 2.2, it may be seen that $1,000,000 of the fixed costs are discretionary and, in fact, avoidable. The segment controllable margin of $2,600,000 indicates that in the short run, the segment is worth continuing. The segment controllable margin should be sufficient to cover the long-run fixed costs if the segment's operations are to be justified in the longer run. In this example, after covering its own long-run nondiscretionary fixed costs, the segment has a net margin of $2,000,000. Failure to cover longer run fixed costs does not necessitate immediate closing of the segment so long as some contribution is made to the costs. However, it might be inferred that in the future as the fixed costs involved become discretionary, the segment should be discontinued.

Note that depreciation is based on the estimated change in market value through continued use (often termed economic depreciation) rather than on an arbitrary allocation of historical cost. This is considered more relevant since the real loss in value through usage is approximated. Historical cost depreciation, which is used for tax and financial reporting purposes, is not relevant for decision making unless it closely approximates the real cost of using the asset.

The statement in Table 2.2 can be converted into the cost-profit-volume chart of Figure 2.2. The forecasted volume is represented by the broken vertical line at the $10,000,000 volume location. The short- and

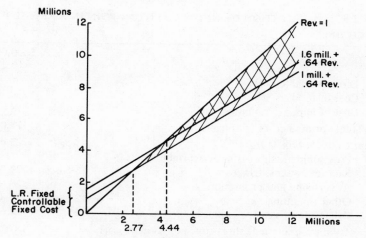

Figure 2.2.   Cost-volume-profit chart.

long-run break-even volumes of $2,770,000 and $4,440,000, respectively, are also charted. The cross-hatched area indicates the net segment margin; the cross-hatched plus diagonal line area shows the segment controllable (short-run) margin. Generally, any decision that maximizes one margin also maximizes the other; however, the differentiation of fixed costs is important in marginal markets where cessation of activities is plausible.

A further example of net segment margin analysis is offered by Table 2.3. A retail fast-food chain analyzes its operations at the store level. Sales at this level are further broken down so that the store manager can determine the contribution margin of the product lines sold. For example, in the illustration of the fast-food chain it is apparent that the sandwich mix contributes $125,000, the jumbo sandwich segment $5,523, and the nonsandwich segment $96,900. These segments could be broken down into more detailed product lines if desired. In this particular company the product lines also can be summed across territory lines in order to determine for geographic areas the amount of raw material that needs to be purchased for each of the product lines sold in a particular area.

CONSIDERING THE INVESTMENT IN THE SEGMENT

The accounting model for segmental analysis must consider the performance of a segment relative to the investment of assets devoted to the

TABLE 2.3   COMPUTATION OF NET SEGMENT MARGIN IN A RETAIL FAST-FOOD CHAIN

Sales	$400,000
Less: Direct variable costs	
Cost of food	$160,000
Cost of paper (wrappings)	18,000
Total variable costs (Controllable)	178,000
Segment Contribution Margin	$222,000
Less: Programmed, short-run, nonvariable costs	
Salaries, wages, fringes	$ 72,800
Advertising and promotion	27,600
Other operating expense	32,800
Other administrative expense	4,000
Total programmed, short-run, nonvariable costs	137,200
Segment Controllable Margin	$ 84,800
Less: Long-run costs specific to segment and allocated to period	
Depreciation—equipment	$ 3,560
Depreciation—store building ($174,200 ÷ 15)*	11,613
Total long-run fixed costs	15,173
Net Segment Margin (before tax)	$ 69,627

	Store		Sandwich Mix Segment		Jumbo Sandwich Segment	
	%	$	%	$	%	$
Sales	100	$400,000	65	$260,000	5.4	$14,000
Cost of food	100	160,000	77	123,000	6.4	7,885
Cost of paper	100	18,000	65	11,700	5.4	632
Segment Contribution Margin				$125,100		$ 5,523

Segment Contribution Margin for Store = $222,000

The contribution margin of nonsandwich segments can easily be determined as $222,000 − $125,100 or $96,900

* Cost to build a store may vary widely with location.

segment if it is to meet the test of optimal use of resources. Two general types of measurement systems are available for this purpose. To explain them, let us resort to a simple example. Let us suppose that a firm invested $100,000 in a segment which is returning a net segment margin of $23,000 per period. Suppose further that the firm has determined that its cost of capital is 15 percent. The most common accounting tool used to relate performance to assets is the return-on-assets (ROA) approach. In this case

$$\text{ROA} = \frac{\text{Net segment margin}}{\text{Specific segment assets}}$$
$$= \frac{\$\ 23{,}000}{\$100{,}000}$$
$$= 23\%$$

An alternative measurement model is offered by the residual income approach first developed by Salmonson. The term "residual" means "after a deduction for the use of capital." In this example, the use of assets would be charged for at a cost of capital rate of 15 percent as follows:

Net segment margin	$23,000
Less: Cost of capital charge	15,000
15% × $100,000 asset value	
Residual segment margin	$ 8,000

Let us consider a more detailed example by applying the alternative measurement tools to the Table 2.2. Just as only specific costs are attached to the segment, only those assets that specifically support the segment's operations are included in the analysis. To make the analysis as relevant as possible, assets are included at their estimated market values. For most short-lived assets, historical cost reasonably parallels market values and thus recorded historical values are typically used for receivables and inventories. However, where inventory values oscillate significantly, current values are preferable. Longer term assets such as plant and equipment can be appraised and included at estimated market values since inflation and technological change invalidate their historical costs for decision purposes. Let us assume the following specific assets:

Inventory	$ 900,000
Receivables (net of specific payables)	1,250,000
Average (during period) estimated market value of plant and equipment	5,000,000
Total specific assets	$7,150,000

Thus:

$$\begin{aligned} \text{ROA} &= \frac{\text{Net segment margin}}{\text{Specific segment assets}} \\ &= \frac{\$2,000,000}{\$7,150,000} \\ &= 28\% \end{aligned}$$

One should be careful to note that ROA traditionally places fully allocated net income over fully allocated assets. Since the measure used here places only net segment margin over specific assets it would probably be best to rename the measure SMOA (segment margin on assets) or some other equally creative label to clearly indicate its unique meaning.

Let us now apply the residual contribution margin model to Table 2.2. The cost of capital is assumed to be 15%. The result is found in Table 2.4. Investment, like costs, has a variable and fixed component. For example, receivables and inventory tend to vary with volume while the investment in plant and equipment remains fixed. With this in mind, Table 2.4 includes the cost of capital charge for inventory and receivables as "variable costs" while the charge for plant and equipment is shown as a fixed cost. A prime advantage of the residual margin approach over ROA models is its ability to place investment costs on equal footing with other recorded costs and to separate the resulting costs according to their behavior. This means that investment can be fitted into the CPV framework as is shown in Figure 2.3. Comparison to Figure 2.2 reveals that the slope of the total cost line is increased by .032 to include the $322,500 variable investment cost. The origin of the long-run total cost line has been increased by $750,000 to include the fixed investment. Note also that the definition of "break-even" must now be changed to mean: "where a segment's revenue covers its specific costs including a charge for assets used." Consequently, short-run break-even becomes sales of $3,050,000 and long-run break-even becomes $7,170,000. Field applications confirm the desirability of this approach. Field managers often tend to maximize the "R" and forget the "A" when making decisions using a ROA model. This is because recorded costs are more obvious than the increase in a segment's asset base at periodic measurement dates. For example, a sales manager may put an item into inventory even where movement is slow. Thus he might warehouse a $20 unit that sells for $25 even if it has a one-year turnover. He will see the $5 increase in his margin more clearly than the indirect

TABLE 2.4 SPECIFIC PRODUCTS DIVISION—RESIDUAL INCOME APPROACH

Revenue		$10,000,000	
Less variable costs			
Out-of-pocket costs from Table 2.2	$6,400,000		
Variable investment charge (based on 15% cost of capital)			
Inventory, 0.15 × $900,000	135,000		(0.0.135 rev.)
Receivables, 0.15 × $1,250,000	187,500		(0.01875 rev.)
Total Variable Costs		6,722,500	(0.67225 rev.)
Segment Contribution Margin			
Less short-run controllable fixed costs			
Same as Table 2.2		1,000,000	
Segment Controllable Margin		2,277,500	
Less long-run fixed costs			
Lease cost, truck fleet	250,000		
Depreciation, plant, & equipment (based on change in market value)	350,000		
Investment in fixed assets, 0.15 × $5,000,000	750,000	1,350,000	
Net Segment Margin (residual income)		$ 927,500	

effect of a $20 increase in his asset base. If, on the other hand, he were charged a cost of capital charge of 15 percent, he could quickly evaluate whether the $5 probable gross profit on the item was worth the likely $3 (0.15 × $20) increase in his cost of capital charge.

In summary, either the ROA or residual income approach can measure the profitability of a segment with the same precision. It is felt, however, that the residual income format simplifies analysis by eliminating one variable, investment, from the "net segment margin model." While the investment variable is removed, it is not ignored; it is merely converted to a cost. Investment is then no longer a second-class citizen analytically since it is put on an equal footing with other costs. A byproduct of the residual approach is the comparability of treatment given to owned and leased fixed assets. Where an asset is leased, the lease payment is listed as an expense. When owned, the expense resulting from asset ownership is economic depreciation plus a cost of

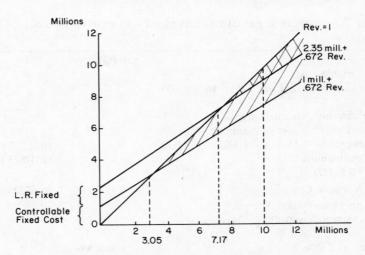

Figure 2.3.   Cost-volume-profit chart (residual income approach).

capital charge based on the asset's average market value during the period. The depreciation plus capital charge will likely approximate a reasonable lease charge. ROA is not consistent in the treatment given leased versus owned assets. Owned assets result in a depreciation charge included in the numerator and the asset's value is included in the denominator. If leased the same asset would result in the lease charge being included in the numerator and there would be no effect on the denominator. Typically this will create a favorable impact on ROA as a result of leasing even though leasing is often more costly than ownership!

There is no doubt that either model can be charged with a lack of comparability when used to compare segments. This is because segments will vary in their relative use of specific versus shared costs and assets. This cannot be denied, yet one must reply with two thoughts:

1. Segmental analysis has as its primary purpose the analysis of potential versus cost so as to maximize profits by segments. It does not seek to level segments. Thus, the test of the model is the degree to which it maximizes contribution by segments, not its ability to be "fair."

2. Is comparability desirable when made possible by arbitrary allocations?

NET MARGIN VERSUS NET INCOME

The model just explained would hold that net income is a term applicable only to an entire firm's performance since only at that level can all costs be attached. Segments are envisioned as only "contributing" to the common costs and profit of the firm.

The segment margin and net income approaches are compared in Figure 2.4. Columns 1 and 2 represent the net income approach and

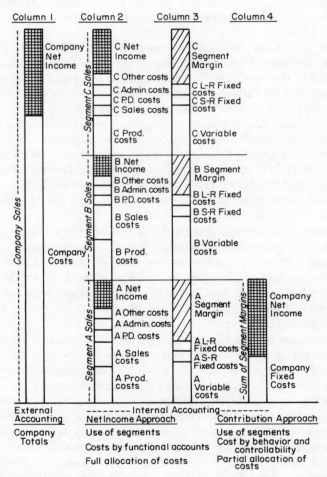

Figure 2.4. Graph comparison of the net income and contribution approaches.

columns 3 and 4 the segment margin approach. Column 1 portrays the external accounting format to total company sales less total expenses equals company net income. Column 2 shows the segmental approach using the fully allocated or net income approach. Sales are divided into selected segments, and functional costs are fully allocated to the segments. The net income for the segments is equal to company net income. For example, in segment A the costs of production, sales costs, physical distribution, administration, and other costs are fully allocated to segment A. The cross-hatched amount in the column represents the net income for the company for segment A. The same is true for segments B and C.

Column 3 depicts the segment margin approach; only the costs directly attributable to the production of segment revenue in a segment are charged to that segment. In each segment the costs are divided into three categories of variable, short-run fixed, and long-run fixed costs. Each segment then produces a net segment margin.

Column 4 shows the summation of segment margins covering common fixed costs and producing net income. The segment margin model further implies a chain of contributions to be analyzed. For example, a customer contributes to a salesman's territory, the territory contributes to a district, and finally the district might contribute to the firm. At each level of the chain, a greater number of costs and assets will become attachable.

The theory here advanced deplores the allocation of common costs, which can only cause confusion and dispute. Those who have used it can typically remember uncovering segments with a "net loss" only to find that, upon further analyses, the profits of the firm would suffer if the segment had not existed. This is because while the segment may not have been covering all common costs allocated to it, it was making a positive contribution to them.

Yet despite the pitfalls of common cost allocation, many firms tremble at the thought of not making each segment responsible for its "fair share" of all costs. Apparently there is a fear that common costs will be forgotten and will go uncovered. The net segment margin approach can accommodate this concern. Common costs are to be covered by determining the reasonable target margin for each segment. After carefully considering a segment's potential it would not be unreasonable to request a minimum acceptable net segment margin. If it is desired this target could be reinforced by reminding the segment of its obligation to cover common costs. Thus, instead of suggesting a $850,000 contribution, one would say, "contribute $400,000 to the fixed costs of the products you sell, contribute $200,000 to corporate overhead, and

TABLE 2.5 SPECIFIC PRODUCTS DIVISION—RESIDUAL INCOME
APPROACH WITH TARGET CONTRIBUTION

Revenue		$10,000,000	
Less variable costs			
Out-of-pocket costs from	$6,400,000		(0.64 rev.)
Table 2.2			
Variable investment charge			
(based on 15% cost of capital)			
Inventory, 0.15 × $900,000	135,000		(0.0135 rev.)
Receivables, 0.15 ×			(0.01875 rev.)
$1,250,000	187,500		
Total Variable Costs		6,722,500	(0.67225 rev.)
Segment Contribution Margin		3,277,500	(0.32775 rev.)
Less short-run controllable fixed			
costs			
Same as Table 2.2		1,000,000	
Segment Controllable Margin		2,277,500	
Less long-run fixed costs			
Lease cost, truck fleet	250,000		
Depreciation, plant, &			
equipment (based on change			
in market value)	350,000		
Investment in fixed assets,			
0.15 × $5,000,000	750,000	1,350,000	
Net Segment Margin (residual income)		927,500	
Less target contribution to corporate common			
costs			
Common production costs	400,000		
Corporate administrative	200,000		
Target income contribution	250,000	850,000	
Net Segment Margin in Excess		$ 77,500	
of Target Contributions			

contribute $250,000 to the firm's net income." Table 2.5 is an example which revises Table 2.3 to include target contributions. The exhibit shows an actual net segment margin $77,500 in excess of the goal. Any such attempt to communicate goals in this manner should, however, make sure that:

1. All common costs are shown below the segment's net segment margin.

2. The allocated common costs are defined as desired levels of coverage and do not represent any real degree of precision as to attachment.
3. It is clearly understood that the costs so allocated are not controllable by the segment. Carefully done, these last-line allocations should help introduce segment margin theory into firms traditionally attached to net income analysis.

CHAPTER 3

AN
Operational System
FOR
Contribution Analysis

An operational system that adequately meets a firm's needs for accounting and financial information must provide for both the external and internal needs of the firm. Traditional accounting systems adequately provide for the external needs. The real need is for an operational system that will also provide for the firm's internal needs.

These internal needs are of two kinds: (1) a knowledge of the relevant functional costs as they are incurred, or shortly thereafter, and (2) the attachment of these functional costs to the relevant segments, here to be deducted from revenue in order to determine the segment's contribution to profit.

The emphasis in this chapter is on developing an understanding of these functional flows and segment costs and revenues and, after developing an adequate understanding of the flows, an operating system is proposed to record this information in a data base. The system should record in such a way that any given data module can be attached on request to the relevant function and/or segment. The form of the inputs into this data base is extremely important, and the last portion of the chapter is an analysis of the factors which will determine these inputs.

FUNCTIONAL COSTS

The normal flow of costs incurred for a product in a manufacturing and distributing firm in a simplistic fashion is as shown in Figure 3.1.

The normal process would consist of acquisition of raw materials obtained outside the company or, if it is vertically integrated, within the firm. These materials are transported to initial production points or stored until production occurs. Then a series of production steps transforms the goods into the forms saleable to the company's markets. Concurrently promotional forces are used to insure that markets are cultivated and sustained. Following production, the goods are moved directly to market or to storage and thence to market.

In each of these activities there are a series of functions that are performed. Each of these functions constitutes an activity center where costs are incurred. These functional cost centers are derived from the principal activity which goes on at each particular point. The planning and control of expenditures largely occurs operationally in these functional centers.

The flow of functional activities will vary with the nature of the business and the markets to be served. For example, in a motor carrier the goods are picked up at the dock of the consignor and moved as a truckload (TL) to the dock of the consignee. No terminal functional costs are involved. Less-than-truckload (LTL) moves are usually picked up at origin and taken to a terminal where the goods are sorted for line-haul movement to the destination terminal. Sorts are made at the destination terminal for delivery to the consignees. More functional cost centers—namely, origin and destination terminals—are involved in LTL than in TL shipments.

The presentation of functional costs in Figure 3.2 is a brief summary of a motor carrier's activities. These in turn contain subcenters, some of which are presented in Table 3.1. The extent to which it is desirable to

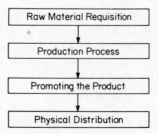

Figure 3.1. Simplistic diagram of cost flows.

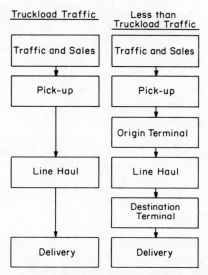

Figure 3.2. Flow of functional costs for truckload and less than truckload traffic.

construct subcenters in the data base will depend on the dollar volume involved and the desired detail of analysis for planning and control. Of course the greater the desired detail, the greater will be the need for the subdivision of functional costs.

The basic question with any functional cost is its attachability to the work being performed. In a sense its attachability is similar to a cafeteria. As an individual passes by alternative foods in a cafeteria line, he selects food and places them on his tray. For each article selected a unit price is provided and the sum total of the unit prices of the foods he selects becomes the total cost of his meal. It is exactly this way with functional costs. The product or service being produced utilizes certain functions with specific unit costs. The functional costs that are used are attached to the product and the sum of these costs are then attached to the appropriate market segment.

The costs as they are incurred at the functional cost level are viewed as either fixed or variable costs. The fixed costs are those costs that are fixed in total for a given level of functional activity and do not vary in total with a change in the level of activity, given a fixed capacity. The variable costs are those that increase with an increase in the volume of activity in the function. The variable costs are more or less constant per unit within a given level of output.

TABLE 3.1 A MOTOR CARRIER'S FUNCTIONAL COST CENTERS

Functional Cost	Variable or Fixed Cost
Line Haul	
Fuel and oil	Variable
Parts, tires, maintenance	Variable
Drivers and helpers	Variable
Taxes and fees	Fixed
Insurance	Fixed
Depreciation and amortization	Fixed
Pickup and delivery	
Fuel and oil	Variable
Parts, tires, maintenance	Variable
Drivers and helpers	Fixed
Taxes and fees	Fixed
Insurance	Fixed
Depreciation and amortization	Fixed
Order processing	
Supervisory and administrative personnel	Fixed
Clerical labor	Variable
Office supplies	Variable
Depreciation and amortization	Fixed
Platform	
Cargo handlers	Variable
Depreciation of service cars and equipment	Fixed
Terminal	
Supervisory and administrative	Fixed
Labor	Variable
General supplies and equipment	Variable
Taxes	Fixed
Insurance	Fixed
Communications and utilities	Variable
Depreciation and amortization	Fixed
Traffic and sales	
Supervisory and administrative	Fixed
Clerical	Variable
Vehicle expenses	Variable
Supplies	Variable
Tariffs and schedules	Fixed
Advertising	Variable
Taxes, fees, insurance	Fixed
Communication	Variable
Insurance and safety	
Labor, clerical, other	Variable
Supplies and general expenses	Variable

The importance of these variable costs is that they become the basis for standard costs for each of the functions. The standard cost, which is a reasonable estimate of per unit cost, is based only on the variable cost of the function since fixed costs are static with respect to output. It is this standard that is attached to the good or service as it is processed through each function.

As the product moves through the production functions into the market the appropriate standard costs can be attached to the marketing segments. Fixed costs would be assigned to the segment only if they were performed for that particular segment. In the hierarchy of marketing segment costs, fixed costs from a function would be attached to the first segment in which the fixed costs would be specifically applicable. If no such segment developed, then the segments would have to be aggregated until such fixed costs were attachable.

An example of functional costs should help us understand the nature of these flows and their relationship to market segments. The example involves a major airline. The airline's major functional cost centers are

1. Flying operations
2. Maintenance/flight equipment
3. Depreciation
4. Customer ticketing
5. Advertising
6. General and administrative

The first three categories of costs are variable costs per flying hour and are attachable to each of the major types of aircraft in use by the company. The other cost categories are considered to be joint costs and are not attachable to particular aircraft types.

Several types of average costs per unit are presented in Figure 3.4. The average cost per flight (block to block) is highest for the B-747 and lowest for the B-737-200; the average hours per flight is five times as long for the B-747 as for the B-737. The B-747 is obviously for long hops (2277 miles) and the B-737 for shorter hops (303 miles).

The average cost per mile flown is not significantly different in the B-727 and B-737 series. The DC-8 also has a relatively low cost per mile.

The expense per flight is also divided into flying cost and ground cost—information that can be used to advantage in route analysis. Other functional cost information available includes hourly depreciation, flight cost per hour, and maintenance/flight equipment per flying hour. Some of these data will be used in the segment contribution analysis.

From the example presented it is possible to use these costs in planning and controlling functional operations. First, activity levels can be forecast and monitored both on a financial and a nonfinancial basis if the data system provides this information on a real-time basis. Standard costs can be used to calculate budgets and monitor variances. The number of physical units processed through the function can supplement the financial information. Second, evaluation of alternative functional combinations to serve given markets can be accomplished through trade-off analyses. Third, comparative analyses can be made between various functions to form performance standards.

NET SEGMENT MARGIN

The flow of functional costs has been presented as a cafeteria of costs in which the product produced or service performed flows through a series of selected functional cost centers. Some functional centers are used and others are not. The sum total of services performed is the production, physical distribution, and marketing cost of the good or service.

All of these goods and services are produced and sold to markets that can be categorized into segments. These segments are classes of products, customers, sizes of orders/shipments, geographic territories, and/or channels of distribution. These are the classical units into which funds flow to the market place with the expectation of output in the form of sales.

As presented in Chapter 2, the difference between the operating revenue of the segment and the input cost to produce that revenue is called net segment margin. The reasons for the value of this approach have been set forth in the previous chapter. The purpose here is to present some examples of how the functional costs relate to net segment margin.

A segment can be any one or more of five categories. Each of these five alternatives has to be operationally defined. In order to help understand this idea, examples are presented. In an example of an airline company the segment is defined as the type of aircraft used and in another example as city pairs.

Average unit costs for plan types are presented in Table 3.2. These costs are compared with the revenue for each type in Table 3.3.

The largest dollar contributor to profit is the B-727-100, but it also earns the largest revenue. Perhaps a better measure of a segment's contribution is its productivity index; this is the aircraft's percent of net segment margin divided by its percent of total revenue. The highest productivity of capital is with the DC-10, followed by the DC-8, and then

TABLE 3.2 TYPES OF AVERAGE UNIT COSTS FOR USE IN ARILINE FUNCTIONAL COSTS

					Plane Type			
Cost	B-727-100	B-727-100QC	B-727-100QCF	B-727-200	B-737-200	B-747	DC-8	DC-10
Operating expenses (000)	$129,559	$ 50,381	$ 11,946	$ 41,159	$ 72,186	$ 66,081	$ 231,287	$ 41,840
Expense per flight	901	886	1,119	783	502	5,990	2,022	2,627
Flying cost per flight	662	640	885	530	310	5,119	1,688	2,077
Ground cost per stop	238	245	234	253	192	871	334	550
Cost per mile	1.014	1.014	1.024	1.025	1.024	2.24	1.32	1.64
Revenue miles (000)	93,943	35,924	9,223	27,186	43,492	25,221	24,114	20,183
Revenue hours	211,261	81,628	19,705	64,251	121,102	48,816	51,156	41,695
Departing flights	143,855	56,844	10,672	52,533	143,776	11,031	1,481	15,925
Av. miles per flight	653	631	864	517	303	2,277	1,264	1,267
Av. hours per flight	1.46	1.44	1.58	1.22	.84	4.4	2.54	2.62
Annual depreciation	15,919	397,088	483,201	483,201	256,119	1,454,469	2,623,382	961,863
Hourly depreciation	55.20	122.39	522.80	174.20	188.98	360.80	85.70	285.09
Capacity	98	98	120	123	90			

TABLE 3.3   SEGMENT CONTRIBUTION TO PROFITS BY AIRCRAFT TYPE

Plane Type	Revenue* (000)	Variable Costs (000)		Fixed Costs Depreciation**	Total Attachable Costs (000)	Contribution by Net Segment Margin (000)	Productivity Index††
		Cost/ Stop†	Cost/ Flight‡				
Company	1,126,538	445	747	80,918	526,665	599,873	
B-727-100	339,257	34,292	95,822	1,161	131,275	207,982	1.15
B-727-100QC	152,677	13,961	36,318	9,990	60,269	92,408	1.14
B-727-100QCF	39,198	2,500	9,445	10,301	22,246	16,952	0.68
B-727-200	115,540	13,305	27,855	11,192	52,352	63,188	1.03
B-737-200	184,841	27,661	44,527	14,408	86,596	98,245	1.00
B-747	106,764	9,608	56,271	17,616	83,495	23,269	0.41
DC-8	102,484	494	31,830	4,364	36,688	65,796	1.21
DC-10	85,777	8,758	33,100	11,886	53,744	32,033	1.34

* Revenue by plane type: average revenue/aircraft mile × revenue miles by aircraft type

† Cost/stop: average cost/stop × no. of departures by type

‡ Cost/flight: average cost/mile by type × total revenue miles by type

** Depreciation: hourly depreciation rate by type × total revenue hours by aircraft type

†† Productivity index = $\dfrac{\text{aircraft contribution} \div \text{total contribution}}{\text{aircraft revenue} \div \text{total revenue}}$

the B-727-100. The poorest producers were the B-747 and the B-727-100QCF (Tables 3.2 and 3.3).

An analysis of the net segment margin by plane type by city pairs will indicate the place of each plane in the company's route structure. This is done for traffic from city X to city Y in Table 3.4. The maximum contribution on this route segment is made by the B-727-100. A negative contribution is made by the B-747. These relationships are shown graphically in Figure 3.3. A horizontal line indicates the expense level association with each type of plan on the segment city X to city Y. The intercept of the cost line and a break-even line indicates on the horizontal line the number of passengers per flight required to break even. As indicated in Table 3.4 the B-727-100 requires the fewest passengers to break even and also makes the greatest contribution at an average load of 67 passengers. The figure also indicates that if loads are larger than average, the contribution may be larger with other types of planes.

Two other examples are presented to show other types of market segments. One is a railroad where the market segments are products

TABLE 3.4   CONTRIBUTION BY PLANE TYPE BY CITY PAIR

	Plane Type				
	B-737-200	B-727-100	B-727-200	B-727-100QCF	B-747
Revenue*	$1608	$1608	$1608	$1608	$1608
Depreciation†	97	40.50	127.80	383.60	255.50
Variable cost‡	394	390.39	394.40	390.30	865.40
Fixed cost**	192	192.30	253.28	245.61	874.44
Total cost††	683	669.27	775.00	1019	1995
Contribution	925	939	833	589	(387)
Break-even point‡‡	28.5	27.8	32	42.5	83
Plane capacity	90	98	123	100	315

All figures are based on the total number of passengers handled by the airline from city X to city Y divided by the number of flights. The costs are based on a distance of just under 400 miles.
* Revenue: revenue/mile × average number of passengers
† Depreciation: hourly rate × flight time
‡ Variable cost: variable cost/mile × air miles
** Fixed cost: fixed cost/stop
†† total cost is sum of all attachable costs
‡‡ Break-even in passengers: total cost ÷ revenue/passenger

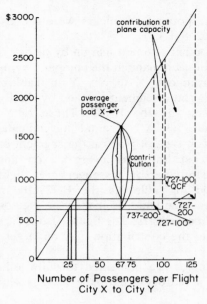

Figure 3.3.   Break-even points on traffic from city X to city Y.

moved by the carrier. The other is sizes of shipments of freight moved by an air freight forwarder.

The railroad uses the principal market categories of farm products, coal, food and kindred products, pulp and paper products, stove and glass products, primary metals, and transport equipment. For this particular carrier these product groupings make it possible to ascertain what categories are making (or not making) contributions to profit and to compare the productivity of capital invested in moving each product category. As shown in Table 3.5 the largest contributors to profit are coal and transportation equipment; the productivity of capital invested was greater for transport equipment than it was for coal.

An air freight forwarder finds it useful to analyze margins by weight groups of goods handled (Table 3.6). The contribution is highest at over 500 pounds per shipment and next highest on shipments under 50 pounds. The productivity of capital is greater, however, on the larger shipments and less productive on the smaller shipments.

The goals of planning and control determine the choice of market segments. As demonstrated in the examples presented in this section there may be a wide variety of goals present in marketing management. The segments chosen must reflect management's desires for adequate segmental data rather than a strait jacket of a single type of segment.

TABLE 3.5 CONTRIBUTION BY PRODUCT GROUP FOR A RAILROAD

Segments	Revenues	Cost Centers			Total Costs	Contri-bution	Contri-bution % of Total	Perform-ance Indicator
		Line Haul Costs	Switching Costs	Station Costs				
Farm products	$ 50,272	$ 15,655	$ 4,348	$ 2,093	$ 22,096	$ 28,176	5.7	1.12
Coal	350,567	152,866	36,647	29,976	218,589	131,978	26.8	0.75
Food and kindred products	74,504	19,952	8,489	1,836	30,277	44,227	9.0	1.18
Lumber and wood products	23,335	6,753	3,106	330	10,189	13,146	2.7	1.13
Pulp and paper products	27,335	6,753	3,416	184	10,353	16,982	3.4	1.21
Chemical products	58,776	15,655	4,762	771	21,188	37,588	7.6	1.27
Stone, clay, and glass products	34,542	13,506	4,762	1,359	19,627	14,915	3.0	0.86
Primary metals	52,658	15,348	4,969	1,652	21,969	30,689	6.2	1.15
Transport equipment	134,402	11,664	10,456	1,102	23,222	111,180	22.6	1.65
Other products	139,446	48,554	22,775	4,957	96,286	63,154	12.8	0.87
Firm totals	945,837	306,960	103,524	43,433	453,917	491,920	100.0	

35

TABLE 3.6 CONTRIBUTION BY WEIGHT GROUPS FOR AN AIR FREIGHT FORWARDER

Weight Breaks (lbs.)	Revenues	Pickup and Delivery Costs	Station Handling Costs	Air Transportation Costs	Total Costs	Contribution	Productivity
0–49	$ 916,449	$470,419	$205,500	$ 150,488	$ 826,408	$ 90,041	0.60
50–99	422,935	128,003	72,116	172,062	372,181	50,754	0.74
100–199	519,912	103,692	75,600	278,602	457,894	62,018	0.73
200–299	331,957	40,931	39,706	189,641	270,278	61,679	1.14
300–399	255,433	22,326	27,084	147,558	196,968	58,465	1.42
400–499	198,835	13,396	19,524	114,797	147,717	51,118	1.55
over 500	2,631,739	48,126	217,859	1,610,353	1,876,338	485,401	1.13
Total	5,277,260	826,893	657,390	2,663,501	4,147,784	859,476	

RECOMMENDED OPERATIONAL SYSTEM FOR COST AND REVENUE FLOWS

An operational system which will provide adequate accounting and financial information must meet both the external and internal needs of the company. The external needs identify summaries of activities in the business which lead to the preparation of balance sheets and statements of profit and loss. The internal needs are for the operation of the functional cost centers and the management of the marketing segments. The internal system requires:

1. Identification of relevant functional cost centers.
2. Establishment of standard costs in each of the cost centers.
3. Identification of relevant marketing segments.
4. Establishment of a system of cost and revenue flows through the functions and into the relevant marketing segments.

With the advent of the computer it has become possible to input this required data in a form where it can be withdrawn on demand on a real-time basis. Former manual and even mechanized accounting and financial procedures required aggregations, sorts, and reaggregations to the point that there were long time lags in the availability of the data relative to the time for its need.

Now it is possible to input information in a data base in a coded form so that it can be retrieved quickly for management decision processes. These coding procedures in a sense create modules of information in a filing system. Each module can be individually retrieved, combined with other modules, and be retrieved in the new form quickly. Lest it be thought that such systems are only for large companies with complex computer systems, the basic idea can be used by the smallest of businesses.

In the recommended information system for cost and revenue flows, provision is made for one input into a modular data base from source documents which should be sufficient to accommodate all needs with analysis on an on-line real-time basis. Figure 3.4 is a diagram of an operational system for cost and revenue flows made possible through the use of a modular data base. The inputted data are coded, so the flows indicated in the diagram become possible. The actual incurred costs flow through the natural accounts and are used for preparing external data; actual costs are also charged to the functional cost centers responsible for their incurrence. As activity occurs in the functional cost centers the

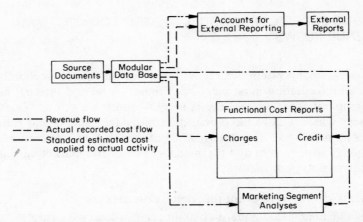

Figure 3.4.   An operational system for cost and revenue flows.

physical units are charged at a standard cost out of the modular data base into the relevant functional cost center. As the good or service moves from the functional cost center to the marketing segment this transfer is made at standard cost (plus any specific fixed cost). The transfers are made by reference to the modular data base.

At the functional cost center level the flows of products from one center to another occur on a real-time basis. Moves to the marketing segments are similarly recorded.

Special procedures need to be developed for inputting promotion costs. Where promotion costs are incurred for a segment by management outside the segment, the segment is charged the budgeted cost. For example, advertising might be centralized as a home office function. In such a case, the advertising is a functional cost center and is accounted for as such. Where, however, promotion costs are incurred directly by the segment being analyzed, actual costs are charged to it so that the segment may compare its own actual and budgeted costs. In summary, the data base charges actual costs only to the function or segment responsible for its original incurrence.

The data base must also assign revenues to the market segment originating the sale. For external reporting, revenue already assigned need only be aggregated. In review the modular data base presented in Figure 3.4 has three basic products:

1. Summaries of the natural accounts for use in preparation of the periodic balance sheet and statements of profit and loss.
2. Functional cost reports comparing actual and budgeted standard cost

for each cost center providing service to market segments. This procedure is already common for production costs but requires expansion to cover physical distribution and centrally incurred promotion costs.

3. Market segment analyses following the net segment margin approach of Chapter 2. Each report subtracts from revenue:

a. the standard budgeted cost of service provided to the segment by functional cost centers. This includes standard variable costs plus any budgeted fixed cost incurred by a function specifically for the sales segment.

b. promotion costs incurred by the segment.

Form of the Modular Data Base

A modular data base is defined as a central data storage system which contains revenue and cost information in readily accessible form. The concept of a modular data base can be visualized in a simplified form for a small jewelry store as shown in Figure 3.5.

The illustration is in three-dimensional form: the horizontal rows indicate product lines, the columns represent store numbers, and the third dimension represents units of time. Each store, product line, and day forms a basic module of data. The columns can then be added to obtain store data or the rows can be summed for overall product-line data. Any combination may be extended over time to get weekly, monthly, quarterly, or annual totals.

While the illustration is simple in three dimensions, the memory system of a computer is capable of recording n dimensions. For example, the product line can be classified into as many segments as the company cares to build into the data base. The same could also be done

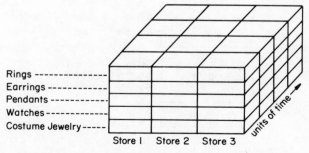

Figure 3.5.   Graphic concept of a modular data base.

for categories of territories, customers, order/shipment sizes, and channels of distribution. Units of time as varied as required for the decision-making process can also be built into the modular data system process.

Coding Revenue and Expense Items into the Modular Data Base

The process of coding revenue and expense items into the modular data base can be a complex process, but the basic ideas are relatively simple. In the left-hand column of Figure 3.6 the desired functions are identified for recording expenses by principal activities of the business. In the illustration these are limited to the functional areas of production, marketing, finance, and physical distribution.

Following the identification of functions, the segments should be identified. In the illustration territories and products are selected as the segments. Certainly other segments would be built into the modular data base if they were desired for purposes of analysis. Each item is then also recorded as to whether it is a revenue or expense item. Expenses are further divided into such subfunction classifications as may be useful.

An example, using the codes indicated in Figure 3.6, shows how a transaction might be coded into the modular data base. Assume a sale of

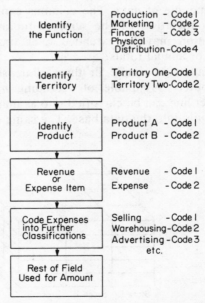

Figure 3.6.   Coding revenue and expense items.

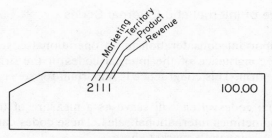

Figure 3.7.   Coding a sale.

product A in territory 1 is to be entered into the data base in the amount of $100. The following code would be used (Figure 3.7): The first figure, number 2, would be marketing; the next, number 1, would indicate territory; the third, number 1, would indicate product; and the fourth, number 1, would indicate revenue. And then in the right-hand part of the card would be $100.

Figure 3.8 shows the recording of an expense of $500 incurred for the advertising of product B in territory 2. The coding would be as follows: The first figure, number 2, indicates marketing; the other figures indicate territory, product, expense, and advertising in the amount of $500.

The above illustrations show how costs and revenues could be attached to a behavioral basis. In the real world, the columnar combinations are limited only by the capacity of the computer and the inventiveness of the individuals concerned. There are many examples of coding systems that run as high as 70 digits and yet maintain a high degree of flexibility of information for decision-making purposes.

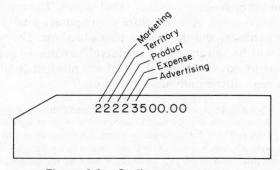

Figure 3.8.   Coding an expense.

Congruence of Internal and External Codes

Another important consideration in an operational cost and revenue system is the congruence of the internal codes of the firm with codes external to the firm. This congruence is important for several reasons:

1. The external codes often will serve as a measure of total domestic sales and sometimes international sales. These codes can be an aid in estimating a company's market share.
2. The external codes may help establish market trends.
3. The external information may aid in assessment of segment life cycles, an important part of market programming.

External codes are available in most of the types of market segments. Some of the external codes available by territory include: U.S. zip codes, U.S. census tracts, individual carrier tariffs, tariffs of the carrier rate bureaus, and standard metropolitan statistical areas. Possibilities for codes in the area of product segments are standard industrial codes, United Nations codes, carrier tariffs and classifications, U.S. Census of Transportation, and codes used in foreign countries. The order size of shipment can commonly be coordinated with the shipment sizes utilized in various carrier tariffs. Customer codes will vary with the line of business of the company, and the possibilities can frequently come from the territory and product codes listed above. Channels of distribution will vary with the channel used for both demand creation and the demand fulfillment; product and territory codes will be useful in setting up channel codes.[1]

The uniform product code appears to offer great possibilities for data congruence. This code consists of a series of market identifications of the package. These markings then provide for automatic checkout at the checkout counter of grocery or other retail stores. The markings on each package are interpreted into the store's computer, a tally made of the customer's purchases, and the transaction added up. The whole process of checkout will be automated. Considerable work is going on at the present time as to ways in which this uniform product coding can be tied into the data base of the individual company.[2]

---

[1] See Appendix B for a more complete description of these external codes.

[2] Some state legislatures have already passed laws that may blunt somewhat the effect of uniform product codes. These forces seem to come from consumer groups who oppose uniform product code labeling because of their inability to compare costs. As a result some state laws require price marks on the product as well as the identifying code marks. Another side-effect of uniform product codes is that it may force the small producers and

FACTORS INFLUENCING SELECTION OF RELEVANT FUNCTIONAL COST CENTERS AND MARKET SEGMENTS

The operating system established to meet internal needs for accounting and financial information assumed the identification of relevant functional cost centers and market segments. This relevancy is important since one must decide in coding for the data base what centers and segments are basic for inputting and outputting of costs and revenues. In this section the major forces are discussed that determine what centers and segments are relevant.

Basically four factors will determine the relevant functional cost centers and market segments:

1. A working definition of present and anticipated future company markets.
2. Knowledge of who makes decisions, what decisions are made, and the needed data for the decision making process.
3. The requisite time frames for each of the decision processes.
4. Flexibility of the system for updating to meet changing data requirements.

Definition of Present and Anticipated Markets

The starting point in the market definition is the decision as to which alternative market segments will be used to categorize revenue. These alternatives are customers, products, territories, order/shipment sizes, and distribution channels. A study by a committee of the American Accounting Association, aimed at assessing the state of the art in financial dimensions of marketing, had this point as one of its objectives.[3] The summary in Table 3.7 shows that product line is the most favored segment, with customer categories second. Sales territories, salesmen, and channels of distribution followed in that order; order size was used by only a few companies.

Provision should be built into the data base for use of alternative segments for future analytical use. As pointed out in Chapter 2, the use

---

manufacturers off the shelf of mass distributors since the labeling may be too expensive for them. Small manufacturers may have to go to specialty stores for distribution channels rather than to mass distributors. Much research needs to be done in the area of uniform product code labeling before generalizations can be made.

[3] The study included 75 of the companies listed in the *Fortune* magazine list of 500 largest U.S. companies.

TABLE 3.7 SEGMENTS FAVORED FOR MARKETING
AND PHYSICAL DISTRIBUTION DECISIONS

	Number of Firms Reporting	Rank
Product line	67	1
Customer	41	2
Sales territories	25	3
Salesmen	20	4
Channels of distribution	19	5
Order/shipment size	8	6

of different segments may be desirable for different markets. At least two instances may give rise to this need. First, different organizational levels in the company may define markets in different ways; for example, a fast-food chain uses sales territories for general operational control but for food purchasing purposes the product categories are used. Second, different segments may be useful in defining a life cycle; the introductory stage of a life cycle may use customer categories to pinpoint innovators using the product whereas at a later marketing state the emphasis may shift to channels of distribution. The point is that from a financial dimensions point of view enough flexibility must be built into the data base to provide for both present and anticipated analytical requirements.

An illustration will show this desired flexibility. Assume the expense and revenue information on two products and four customers in two territories, as shown in Table 3.8. The data are presented for two years.

The gross variable margin and net segment margin are shown for the two years in Table 3.9. It becomes apparent when the data are presented by product that A earns a great deal more in terms of segmental contribution margin than does product B. Its segment contribution is 14 percent of sales as compared to 0.6 percent for product B. When summarized by territory, territory 2 appears as a more productive territory in terms of segmental contribution margin percentage than does territory 1. When classified by customers, it is customer 4 that is the most profitable; customer 2 ranks lowest.

In order to provide an additional understanding of the possibilities for flexibility, the gross variable margins and the net segment margins have been arranged by customer and product categories in rank order. The customer product mix of 1-A, 2-A, and 4-A are all very good. The

TABLE 3.8   ILLUSTRATIVE SEGMENTAL REVENUE AND EXPENSE DATA

| | Territory 1 | | | | Territory 2 | | | |
| | Customer 1 | | Customer 2 | | Customer 3 | | Customer 4 | |
	Year 1	Year 2	Year 1	Year 2	Year 1	Year 2	Year 1	Year 2
Product A								
Sales	$20,000	$22,000	$10,000	$9,000	$15,000	$17,000	$30,000	$31,000
Cost of goods	12,000	13,100	6,000	6,355	9,000	10,115	18,000	18,445
Gross variable margin	8,000	8,900	4,000	3,645	6,000	6,885	12,000	12,555
Personal selling	1,500	1,600	750	750	1,200	1,500	2,000	2,500
Advertising & promotion	1,000	1,100	500	500	800	1,000	1,800	2,200
Transportation	500	550	300	275	400	450	850	875
Warehousing & handling	500	550	260	250	375	425	750	775
Credit & collections	200	220	200	180	175	200	400	410
Distribution finance	200	210	100	100	150	175	600	620
General distribution	1,000	1,000	500	500	750	800	1,500	1,550
Net Segment margin	$ 3,100	$ (50)	$ 1,390	$1,090	$ 2,150	$ 2,335	$ 4,100	$ 3,625
Product B								
Sales	$75,000	$100,000	$60,000	$80,000	$60,000	$72,000	$110,000	$140,000
Cost of goods	54,750	75,000	43,800	60,000	43,800	54,000	80,300	105,000
Gross variable margin	20,250	25,000	16,200	20,000	16,200	18,000	29,700	35,000
Personal selling	7,500	8,500	6,500	7,000	6,000	7,000	9,500	10,500
Advertising & promotion	5,000	6,500	4,000	5,000	4,000	4,500	6,000	7,500
Transportation	1,500	2,000	1,300	1,740	1,290	1,560	2,600	2,900
Warehousing & handling	1,500	2,000	1,260	1,670	1,400	1,680	2,650	3,000
Credit & collections	300	1,000	500	670	700	750	1,000	1,200
Distribution finance	750	950	500	675	550	650	950	1,100
General distribution	3,500	4,000	2,500	3,100	2,700	3,200	4,200	4,900
Net segment margin	$ (300)	$ (50)	$ (350)	$ 145	$ (440)	$(1,340)	$ 2,800	$ 3,900

Source. Furnished through the courtesy of Professor Leo G. Erickson, Professor of Marketing, Michigan State University.

TABLE 3.9   SUMMARY OF MARGINS

	Gross Variable Margin (%)		Net Segment Margin (%)	
	Year 1	Year 2	Year 1	Year 2
Product A	40.0	40.5	14.3	13.4
Product B	27.0	25.0	0.6	0.7
Territory 1	29.4	27.3	2.3	2.3
Territory 2	29.7	27.9	4.0	3.3
Customer 1	29.7	27.8	2.9	3.0
Customer 2	28.9	26.4	1.5	1.4
Customer 3	30.7	28.0	2.3	1.1
Customer 4	29.8	27.8	4.9	4.4

contribution from product B is low for customers 1 and 3, and would merit some investigation by the segment manager (Table 3.10).

Similar alternative combinations could be utilized by the segment managers at all levels in the company to use these data as a basis for market planning and control. The purpose of the illustration is simply to demonstrate that the operating system must be flexible enough to permit aggregation and reaggregation of the elements in the system.

The Decision-Making Process

Improved planning and control is the result of an improved decision-making process. Therefore it is important to understand who makes decisions at each organizational level, the specific decisions made, the desired data for the decision-making process, and how often the data are required. An instance of a small retail chain will illustrate who the decision makers are, the decisions they make, and within what time frames. In addition to the owner, there is one manager who is responsible for all three stores. Each store has an assistant manager. The relative participation of each of the individuals in the decision-making process is shown in Table 3.11.

The decisions are quite commonly those that might be made in any marketing or distribution activity, particularly retailing. One can see that the owner has certain decisions where he has a high responsibility. The manager has his areas of responsibility and the assistants have very little responsibility except for scheduling substitutions. The time frames also indicate the frequency of decision. The information shown above was very helpful in setting up a simplified data system.

TABLE 3.10 RATIOS BY CUSTOMER-PRODUCT

Customer Product	Gross Variable Margin	Net Segment Margin	Sales	Gross Variable Margin as % of Sales	Net Segment Margin as % of Sales
1-A-year 2	$ 8,900	$ 3,570	$ 22,000	0.405	0.162
2-A-year 2	3,645	1,090	9,000	0.405	0.121
3-A-year 2	6,885	2,335	17,000	0.405	0.137
4-A-year 2	12,555	3,625	31,000	0.405	0.117
1-B-year 2	25,000	– 50	100,000	0.250	–0.001
2-B-year 2	20,000	145	80,000	0.250	0.002
3-B-year 2	18,000	–1,340	72,000	0.250	–0.018
4-B-year 2	35,000	3,900	140,000	0.250	0.028

TABLE 3.11   DECISION-MAKERS IN A SMALL RETAIL CHAIN

	Decision Levels			Time Frames (frequency of decision)
	Owner	Manager	Ass'ts.	
Adding or deleting a store	Hi	Lo	None	As needed*
Adding or deleting a product line	Med	Hi	Lo	As needed*
Changing product mix	Med	Hi	Lo	Semiannually
Merchandising buying	Hi	Med	None	Monthly
What items to mark down	Lo	Hi	Lo	Semiannually
How much to mark down items	Lo	Hi	Lo	Semiannually
Scheduling of employees	None	Hi	Med	Weekly
Schedule substitutions	None	Lo	Hi	Daily, as needed

* With the proposed controls for variance supported by the modular data base providing timely segmental information, product line and store reviews could easily be programmed for regular intervals.

In order to get a general understanding of the state of the art, the American Accounting Association in its study selected five decision areas from marketing and physical distribution and related these to the decision levels of salesman, sales territory, department, division, and corporate. Somewhat surprisingly, as shown in Table 3.12, in terms of numbers of decisions made, the departmental level makes the most decisions and the division level is second. Third choice was spread throughout all decision areas and levels. No inference can be made with respect to the quality of the decisions since the questionnaire only asked

TABLE 3.12   TYPE OF DECISION BY DECISION LEVEL

	Sales-man	Sales Territory	Depart-ment	Division	Corpo-rate
Sales forecasting	4	3	1	2	3
Planning the promotional mix	5	4	1	2	3
Planning physical distribution mix	5	4	1	2	3
Budgeting	5	3	1	2	4
Variance analysis	4	3	1	2	4

for the number of decisions that were made in each of the types of five decisions by administrative level. Of course, though the decisions at the corporate level may be more important from a planning point of view, most decisions are made at the department level.

The types of decision made were arbitrarily limited in the study to the five indicated. The frequency of request for data is indicated in Table 3.13. It is apparent that sales forecasting is a field for which data are frequently requested. This was followed by budgeting and variance analysis, both of which are important in accounting and in financial systems. Both promotional and distribution mix planning were considerably lower in the number of responses.

The choice of segment within each decision category was for product categories first and customers second. The response was mixed for the other three segmental alternatives.

Influence of Time

Another factor influencing the information system is the need for data within adequate time frames for planning and control. Respondents to the American Accounting Association survey were asked to check how frequently they require information in each of the types of decision areas to check whether they required the information daily, weekly, monthly, quarterly, or yearly. The results are shown in Table 3.14.

The yearly requirement for data was number one in all categories. This preference for the one-year time period probably reflects the impact of financial accounting since most external accounts are prepared on an annual basis. Number two in most areas was quarterly, but in variance analysis it was monthly. An interesting side comment is that in many instances daily information on specific order or product pricing was

TABLE 3.13 TOTAL REQUESTS FOR DATA BY
TYPE OF DECISION

Type of Decision	Total Requests	Rank
Sales forecasting	611	1
Planning the promotional mix	378	5
Planning the physical distribution mix	388	4
Budgeting	491	3
Variance analysis	506	2

TABLE 3.14   INFORMATION NEEDS BY TIME PERIOD

Type of Decision	Daily	Weekly	Monthly	Quarterly	Yearly
Sales forecasting	5	4	1*	3	1*
Planning the promotional mix	5	4	3	2	1
Planning physical distribution mix	5	4	3	2	1
Budgeting	5	4	3	2	1
Variance analysis	5	4	2	3	1
Specific order of product pricing	2	5	3	3	1

* Tie

required by a great many companies; in fact, it was second choice in that type of decision.

Other Factors Affecting the Information System

Other factors that need to be considered in establishing an information system on cost and revenue are the following:

1. Emphasis may be limited to key accounts. The almost universal application of the 20/80 principle exemplifies the fact that 20 percent of the customers account for 80 percent of the company's business. There are many instances in which this same statement could be made with respect to product categories, order size, territories, and perhaps even channels of distribution. In any case, the emphasis may be given to primary accounts of the business enterprise, with only secondary consideration given to the smaller accounts or segments.

2. One of the primary considerations in any modular data system are the cost-benefit considerations involved in establishing the system. Certainly costs must be balanced off against the benefits to be derived in making the data available for better decision-making through better planning and control.[4] This is well understood in accounting for production costs. Many firms find it prohibitively expensive to analyze each element of cost as to its behavior thus they combine all such small items into one group of costs termed "overhead." The cost of production overhead as an aggregate is then studied as to its

---

[4] For problems involved in the costing of computer systems, see William F. Sharpe, *Economics of Computers* (New York: Columbia University Press, 1969).

behavior. Similar aggregation may be needed for nonproduction costs.

3. Some consideration should be given to the amount of information required for special projects. It may be that in many instances these requirements can be anticipated and provisions made for them in construction of the modular data base.

4. A very real difficulty is the feasibility of attaching costs to particular segments. In some cost categories the segments may have to be joined together before costs can be identified with the revenue produced. However, many companies have already gained considerable experience in attaching costs to particular segments. This is particularly true of those companies that have followed the traditional full-costing net-income approach and have developed rather sophisticated means of allocating costs to particular segments. Though one cannot agree with a full allocation of even fixed costs, the allocation factors may present a logical behavior pattern for variable costs. This experience can be of considerable help in setting up the information system.

5. The operating philosophy of the firm and the competitive philosophy of the industry may also be factors worthy of consideration. It may be important that the modular data base be capable of relating data to problems involving percent of market, price leadership, or price lining.

CHAPTER 4
Forecasting
AND
Monitoring
Markets

Effective implementation of the segment contribution approach requires, antecedently, short-term, intermediate, and long-term marketing plans, and these, in turn, depend on precise forecasting of revenues, costs, and relevant technological changes.
If the segment contribution approach is to be effectively implemented, the company must establish a means of forecasting and monitoring its markets on a continuing basis with respect to revenues, costs, and technological changes. Forecasting is needed as an input for plans; monitoring is required for effective control. Markets are dynamic, not static. Hence a "moving picture" rather than periodic still photographs must be provided for this dual purpose.

REVENUE FORECASTING

In the short-term plan the concern is with predicting sales. Companies in different industries vary considerably on what constitutes a useful time-horizon for such immediate projections—the clothing manufacturer may need to look two seasons ahead while the restaurateur may require only a weekly forecast. Generally speaking, for short-term forecasting trend

52

analysis is adequate. Illustratively, each salesman of the clothing manufacturer may be asked to forecast sales in his territory, by account and
by category of goods. The district sales manager may temper these
estimates on the part of each salesman and aggregate them in a district
forecast. The national sales manager may, in turn, temper and aggregate
the district data. The restaurateur may make a menu analysis of last
week's sales and from such information project next week's patronage.

Intermediate and long-term forecasts require attention to contingency
factors that may intervene. Often projections are made in terms of
minimal, likely, and optimal conditions. Also, sales projections in the
longer term require a three-fold frame of reference for their interpretation: marketing (total business likely to be available to the company and
all its competition), economic (projected national, regional, or local
business conditions depending on the scope of the firm's markets), and,
more broadly, environmental (likely stance of government, changes in
life styles, demographic shifts, etc.).

Figure 4.1 depicts these projections. Such data can be inferred from
various secondary sources such as USDC *Industrial Outlook* and other
government publications, bank letters, and industry-sponsored studies.
Each firm, however, should augment published data with market and
sales projections of its own.

Two market conditions put a premium on trustworthy *economic*
information. First, if demand is derived rather than direct, the firm's
sales will fluctuate with economic conditions. Second, if purchases of
the firm's product represents discretionary expenditures, postponement
may be a special problem. (Hedge purchasing may also be a contingency
to look out for.)

Marketers of consumer products must pay special attention to *demo-*

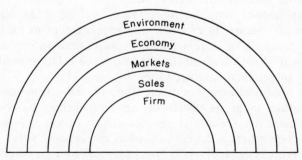

Figure 4.1. Needed frames of reference for intermediate and long-term
forecasting.

graphics. Such data will influence the design of product offerings, the means used to cultivate demand, and the delineation of markets. This is a critical consideration if the firm espouses a *market-segmentation*, as opposed to a *product-differentiation*, strategy—that is, if it opts to customize its line, market by market, rather than to rely on heavy promotion to move a limited line to all its markets. Incidentally, market segmentation as a strategy requires sufficient ongoing demand in each of the firm's markets to insure economies of scale in production of customized offerings. Product differentiation requires a well-conceived promotional effort based on detailed insight regarding each market segment's needs and an analysis of competitive offerings and strategies.

Every company must have data about its *competitors*. After all, *differential competitive advantage* is a universal corporate strategic objective. For any significant purchase the market member's perspective is comparative. He seeks the "best buy" among the options available. One of the inputs, then, for marketing is a thorough knowledge of competitive products and strategies.

Broadly construed, *psychographics* encompass relevant data for understanding the answers to these basic questions. What are the characteristics of market members? What motivates market members to buy? What should the firm do or avoid doing in fostering favorable relationships with market members?

Financial data include comprehensive cost/revenue/profit information. This category is the main thrust of this book and is a crucial ingredient in establishing a comprehensive marketing information system (MIS).

Sound financial data become extremely important for *planning, deciding,* and *acting* as profits erode and growth is curtailed. Such information must meet the tests of *accuracy, specificity*, and *timeliness*. It is self-evident that inaccurate cost/revenue data can lead to botched plans, poor decisions, and unwarranted actions.

Specificity implies that the information will be disaggregated sufficiently to meet the needs of marketing management at all levels. It is difficult to conceive of decentralized decision-making in the marketing organization if those involved do not know the relative contribution to profitability of products and accounts.

The very tempo of business dictates the need for timeliness. Marketing information must be available on a real-time basis. Historical retrieval of data may render it obsolescent or obsolete in today's fast-moving markets where a delayed decision can prove costly.

Multiple regression analysis is the statistical tool commonly used for such inhouse longer term forecasting. It takes the form:

$$Y = b_1 x_1 + b_2 x_2 + b_3 x_3 \cdots + A$$

where Y is what is to be predicted (e.g., market share, the dependent variable), x_1, x_2, x_3 $\cdots$ are the predictors (the independent variables), b_1, b_2, b_3 $\cdots$ are regression weights, and A is the regression constant (a function of the predictors used).

A key consideration in intermediate and long-term forecasts is to find "lead" variables—that is, predictors whose current behavior predicts the dependent variable at the desired future time. This allows for necessary marketing accommodations. For example, a 24-month lead time may be needed to design and manufacture a product. As another example, building a sales force to cope with an impending market change may be a two- or three-year projection.

Such statistical studies are not likely to predict disaggregated information; rather, they generally encompass large markets and broad product groups.

It is important to note that both "bottom-up" trend analysis and "top-down" statistical forecasting assume continuity of data. When discontinuity occurs due to natural calamity, war, sudden technological breakthrough, or other causes, long-term projections are quickly invalidated.

Another important consideration in making statistical forecasts is that a linear relationship is assumed between predictors and what is predicted. In given situations, significant curvilinear relationships may exist which are not manifest in linear computations.

Also, in markets where demand is derived, it is crucial to consider in forecasts the variables of factors on which demand depends—for example, consider the dependency of pleasure travel on availability of discretionary income or sale of automobile tires on car output.

COST FORECASTING

Revenue forecasts are not very helpful unless they are combined with forecasts of costs. Through the proper consideration of costs and revenues the contributions of the segments can be tuned to maximize the future profits of the firm. To accomplish this combining of cost and revenue, the modular data base must be used on a pro forma basis. (In Chapter 7 we will make the point that each functional cost center must predict its costs for future periods so that it can establish a budget). The budget will state the per-unit and fixed costs for the desired future time horizon. Once these budgeted costs are entered into the data base the cafeteria of costs needed to charge market segments is available. A new dimension may, however, be added to the budgeting process. For each segment a forecast of the use of physical distribution services as well as centrally incurred promotion costs must be added to the projected number of units to be sold. Thus, if for each segment unit sales are forecast along with the projection of the use of nonproduction functional services, contribution forecasts can be quickly prepared; this allows several alternative forecasts to be tested for their contribution impact.

The difficult task is the prediction of the functional costs themselves. In the short run these costs can be predicted inferentially by reference to relevant survey data published by government and industry groups and by trend analysis within the company. In the intermediate and long term, attention must be directed to economic and industry forecasts and to likely technological developments which may affect production costs as well as demand for the firm's output. The rapidity of technological changes can markedly influence the time horizon for capital commitment and consequently the cost of capital. On a positive note, technological breakthroughs often result in increased efficiencies and resulting cost reductions.

Companies heavily dependent on natural resources need to monitor the sources of supplies, especially impending shortages and cartel-controlled prices. Petroleum is a dramatic illustration of both these factors.

TECHNOLOGICAL FORECASTING

In virtually every business both revenue and cost projections will be influenced by technological changes and developments. These can affect internal processes as well as the use of the firm's offerings in each of its markets.

A different approach is required for technological forecasting than for either costs or revenues. Judgment of special "knowers" in each relevant field or discipline is the key input. Such persons review the present state of the art and identify the key unanswered questions and the unfulfilled needs. They then make estimates of when developments will take place. This can be systematized using the Delphi method. Essentially, a panel of "knowers" drawn from within and perhaps from outside the company is asked to state what developments are imminent and when they will occur. The opinions are collated and a summary is sent to each panel member asking that he review the proposed list and timetable of developments and that he amend the data and place a probability figure on each entry. This procedure is iterated until near-consensus is achieved.[1]

[1] See Gerald M. Estes and Don Kuespert, "Delphi in Industrial Forecasting," *Chemical and Engineering News*, August 23, 1976, pp. 46–47.

DEDUCTIVE APPROACH TO FORECASTING

The deductive approach to forecasting proceeds from the general to the specific. It is the most commonly used approach to making forecasts for business and government. As an example the automobile industry in the United States goes through the following process in making forecasts for the sales of its products domestically:

1. A correlation is established between gross national product (GNP) and national expenditures on domestic transportation of all kinds. GNP is established as the lead series, and transportation expenditure is the lag series.
2. A forecast is made of GNP and of the resultant amount expended on domestic transportation.
3. Based on a historic percentage of a company's participation in domestic transportation expenditures and anticipated changes in corporate policy, a given percentage is established as going to a particular company.
4. Estimates are made of the amount of the company's business that will go to given body lines.
5. Estimates are made of the percentages of given body lines going to given markets.

The strength of this approach lies in the reliability of aggregate statistics—that is, errors of estimate tend to cancel each other out. Thus, when we make a forecast for the economy as a whole and proceed to the forecast for the industry, the aggregates tend to be reasonably reliable in the short tun (Figure 4.2).

As one proceeds to a recognition of the internal constraints of the company, both in terms of its policies and its abilities to participate in total transportation expenditures, the aggregates begin to be less reliable and more subjective.[2] And then as we proceed to go to the forecast of the segments of the firms, and particularly to margin standards and profit standards, the weaknesses of the deductive approach illustrate great inability to forecast accurately for specific market segments.

[2] This is the result of several factors: (1) The more disaggregated, the narrower the data base, and, as a result, the smaller the number of "cases." Generally speaking, reliability is a function of $1/n$; in the extreme, as $n = 1$, chance effect can range from 0 to 1. (2) Also, the more disaggregated, the more subjective is the classification scheme.

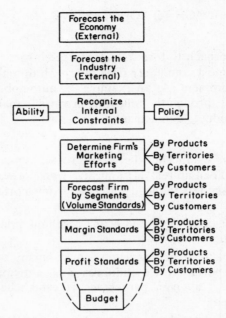

Figure 4.2. Steps involved in the forecasting process. Adapted from Richard J. Lewis and Leo G. Erickson, "Distribution Costing: An Overview," *Distribution Systems Costing: Concepts and Procedures* (Columbus, Ohio: Fourth Annual James R. Riley Logistics Symposium, 1972) p. 15A.

INDUCTIVE APPROACH TO FORECASTING

The inductive approach to forecasting basically starts with the forecast for specific segments and sums them together into a general forecasting procedure. The deductive approach starts from the top of the chart and goes down to the specific at the bottom of the chart. The inductive approach starts at the segmental level and proceeds up to the top of the chart.

In order to proceed reasonably accurately with the inductive approach, let us start first with the definition of *demand*. Basically, the definition of demand involves a definition of the *buying unit*, determination of the number of buying units, location of the buying units, determination of ability to buy, and the presence of willingness to buy.

A company's definition of the buying unit is extremely important for it will in large part determine the segments to be used for analytical purposes. What may appear to be widely different and incongruous definitions of customers may, in actual fact, be the market for the product. For example, a company manufacturing a general industrial line of power tools had this list of customers in one geographic sales area: engineering construction, lumber construction, iron foundry, conveyor belt builder, and a road machinery builder. This particular firm was also interested in selling to the residential construction industry in a particular market. So it included firms in this industry as a part of the definition of the buying unit. The need for flexibility in defining the buying unit in alternative circumstances needs to be built into the modular data base.

Illustrative Use of Inductive Approach

The segmental forecast under the inductive approach can be done in two parts: (1) an evaluation of present accounts, and (2) an estimate of likely results in potential accounts. Pertinent illustrations involve use of such data in analyzing the cost of the selling effort. For industrial firms, personal selling is a major cost category in generating and sustaining demand. Further, typically only about 20 to 25 percent of the salesman's working time is spent face to face with those in a position to buy. Thus each such unit of time is extremely costly.

One financial approach is to calculate contributions of such segments in terms of input sales call hours. In Table 4.1 a company is shown that sells a general industrial line of power tools. We will limit our discussion to a particular sales district. The products sold to each of the customers in the district and the variable cost per unit are shown for marketing and physical distribution. The contribution is the remaining part of the revenue dollar after variable costs are covered. Therefore revenue minus variable costs would give contribution on each product sold to each customer. The total dollar amount of contribution divided by sales call hours gives the contribution per sales call hour.

One can note those accounts where it may be possible to increase or decrease sales call hours in order to increase the productivity of the salesman. Three such illustrations might be Beta Foundry, Rockaway Conveyors, and Hammond Equipment. The contribution per call hour is relatively low in the sale of machine tools to Beta Foundry, and also to Rockaway Conveyors; certainly some serious consideration should be given to decreasing the number of sales hours devoted to selling machine tools to Rockaway Conveyors, particularly since 52 hours have been spent in the past period with relatively low productivity per sales call hour. On the other hand, some increases might be appropriate in the sale of compressors to Hammond Equipment which has a relatively good

TABLE 4.1 CONTRIBUTION IN TERMS OF SALES CALL INPUTS

| Customer Company | Product Sold | Variable Cost Per Unit | | Contribution Per Unit | Sales to Customer | Contribution | Sales Call Hours | Contribution Per Sales Call Hour |
		Mktg.	PD					
Oak Engineering	Power tools	$.50	$.05	$.45	$ 5,100	$ 2,295	5	$459
ABC Builders	Power tools	.50	.05	.45	1,200	540	2	270
Beta Foundry	Machine tools	.70	.10	.20	2,500	500	3	167
	Compressors	.60	.08	.32	1,250	400	1	400
Rockaway Conveyors	Compressors	.60	.08	.32	21,000	6,720	25	269
	Machine tools	.70	.10	.20	41,500	8,300	52	160
Johnson Road Machinery	Pumps	.60	.09	.31	35,000	10,850	30	362
	Power tools	.50	.05	.45	11,000	4,950	15	330
Rodney Iron Works	Machine tools	.70	.10	.20	25,000	5,000	13	385
Hammond Equipment	Compressors	.60	.08	.32	57,000	18,240	54	338
							200	

productivity per sales call hour in spite of the very large number of sales calls made on that particular company.

It should be noted that the only purpose in this analysis is to note possible improvements in the salesman's use of his time as a scarce resource. This measure should not in any sense be used as a quota or as an absolute measure in any one time period. Certainly there are circumstances that the individual salesman and perhaps his supervisor know of that justify continued calls upon particular accounts or in particular product lines with the hope of an order in the near future. It does serve, however, to focus on those points where special attention might be given to reallocating the salesman's time to improve his productivity.

For each customer we might proceed with a matrix approach to see if more sales effort on a particular account would pay off. The matrix for a particular customer might look like Table 4.2.

The salesman might be used as a source of information to obtain from a given customer, if possible, his total purchases of a given kind of product in a given time period and the company's estimate of what their sales might look like in the future time periods for that particular product. Of course, we can get the sales that we have made from our own records, and we should be able to calculate the contribution on that particular product sold to that particular customer. We might then be able to make a more intelligent judgment on whether or not we wish to change our marketing effort with respect to that particular customer.

The second part of the segmental forecast is to evaluate potential accounts. The definition of buying unit can come from the company's records converted into SIC numbers. For example, the industrial power tool manufacturer compiled a list of all customers from its own records utilizing the SIC codes. Of course, the company had integrated its own product codes with the SIC codes.

TABLE 4.2 ESTIMATE OF MARKET AND SALES POTENTIAL AND TRENDS

	Past	Future	Trend
Total customer purchase of a given product	Market	Potential market	Up or down
Our sales of the product to the customer	Sales	Potential sales	Up or down
Our share of the business	Market share	Potential market share	Penetration

The location of the buying units can be achieved through the use of Dun and Bradstreet directories (for example, the Million Dollar Directory) or similar directories for their products. The firms are shown in the Dun and Bradstreet directories by SIC code for principal product of manufacture by census district. From the company's list of customers by SIC code and D&B's list, a list of prospects was obtained. The persons doing this for some other industry might use their imagination by simply referring to such things as trade directories, purchasing catalogs, or whatever kind of directory proves useful for their particular purpose.

The ability to buy of these potential accounts was obtained by using Dun and Bradstreet's financial rating assigned to the particular firm. It was arbitrarily decided that below a certain credit level the power tool manufacturer was not interested in selling to that particular type of client.

The particular kind of buying unit is harder to come by. This may have to be obtained by direct call by the salesman, or through an educated guess by the market researcher, or both. In any case, it is very subjective and hard to estimate.

Willingness to buy depends, of course, on the extent to which the company wishes to devote resources in penetrating the market. This could be simply taking effort away from present accounts and devoting it to new potential accounts through the efforts of the individual salesman. Or it might go so far as to involve the company in a decision to penetrate a whole new market; here again, this is a very subjective decision on the part of management. However, with the modular data base there is information on which to plan a little more rationally than otherwise might be the case. This is particularly true when the information in the modular data base is correlated with external sources, and it becomes possible to calculate actual or potential contribution margins on both present and potential customers.

A Summary of Customer-Prospect Mix and Product-Service Mix Interaction

The third part of the segmental forecast is to bring together the forecast made in both the deductive and inductive approaches. A summary of the anticipated effort by segment should be constructed from the combined approaches. This is depicted in Figure 4.3a. The columnar sums give the anticipated sales by segments. The row sums are the summation of product service offerings to the market segments

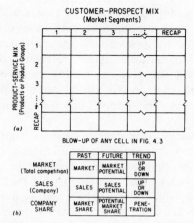

Figure 4.3. Customer-prospect mix and product-service mix interaction.

covered in the figure. Finally, a recap of both rows and columns provides a picture of total business across all segments.

Note that *all* cells when blown up would contain data as depicted in Figure 4.3*b*. Note also that cost data may be inserted in the sales cells to show actual and potential contribution.

Since the deductive approach has a great deal of value when applied to aggregates, this approach should be used to double-check the forecast built up on the individual segments. If everything worked ideally, the deductive and inductive would meet in total in the figure proposed above.

CALCULATION OF SALES POTENTIALS

Potential is defined as the absolute or relative maximum capacity of segments of a buyer's side of the market to purchase a specific type of offering in a specified time. It refers to the maximum capacity of various market segments to purchase a given offering, and the assumption is made that purchasers in each segment of the market have adequate opportunity to know about and purchase the offering. Consequently, potential is not influenced by the variations in the seller's activities in the market during the time period. It represents the maximum that could be sold under ideal selling conditions. In Lewis and Erickson's terms, potential consists of "consuming units with money willing to spend." [3]

Potential does refer to a specific time period and to a specified geographic market. Furthermore, it has reference to an assortment of offerings that the buyer perceives as having a very high cross-elasticity of demand. Potential, therfore, is the relative opportunity to sell by segments of the business. This opportunity is realistic in the present time period.

There are two notions of opportunity—present opportunity and future opportunity. Future opportunity is a probabilistic approach to market determination. Present opportunity is deterministic.

Sales potential deals with the present in that the market is of a fixed size and composition; sales potential measures a market as it exists. There is nothing that the seller can do to alter the market as it exists in the present. Thus, marketing potential of a segment is deterministic and measures the relative opportunity of the firm to sell its products or services.

The role of sales potential in the planning and controlling of marketing activities is illustrated by Lewis and Erickson.[4] They view planning and control as having three supports: cost data, revenue data, and sales potential.

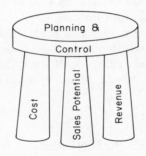

Costs are the physical distribution and marketing functional efforts necessary to get the goods to the right segment, at the right place, at the right time, and in the right quantity; the individuals concerned with cost tend to think of themselves as cost centers attempting to minimize total costs. On the revenue side, the emphasis tends to be on maximizing of

[3] Richard J. Lewis and Leo G. Erickson, "Distribution Costing: An Overview," *Distribution System Costing: Concepts and Procedures* (Columbus, Ohio: Fourth Annual James R. Riley Logistics Symposium, 1972), pp. 1–30.

[4] *Ibid.*, pp. 15–16.

revenues. Sales potential is the balancing leg which provides a standard for planning and control of cost inputs as related to revenue outputs.

An effective method for estimating sales potential is presented by Leo Erickson. The procedure is presented graphically in Figure 4.4. The starting point is to identify measures of buying or consuming units with the ability and with the willingness to buy. The buying or consuming units may be population, household units, or other consuming units such as industrial buyers. The data needed of these consumer units are the units with the ability and the willingness to buy. Without these last two items—purchasing power and willingness to buy—no matter how large the consuming units are there is little or no potential at all. Published

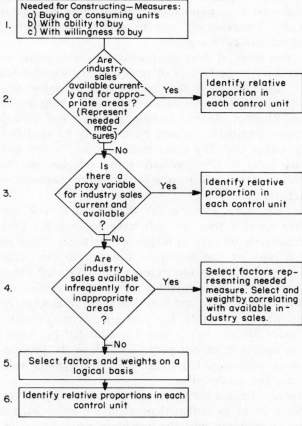

Figure 4.4. Constructing sales potentials.

information is available from the U.S. Census reports, U.S. Department of Commerce reports, trade association reports, and other sources to help define adequate basic measures.

The second step is to obtain total industry sales of the particular product in question at the appropriate segmental levels. For example, if we are estimating sales potential in the Chicago area, we would like to know exactly the total sales of the product (including our own) within the Chicago area. Statistics can be obtained from reports published by the U.S. Department of Commerce, by trade associations, or by special surveys. These reports and statistical abstracts contain complete industry sales with the latest figures for the appropriate area.

In the second step, if the industry sales are available currently for the appropriate segments, it is possible to identify (or calculate) the relative proportion in each segment. Thus we may discover Cleveland has 1 percent of the total U.S. population, yet we sell 4 percent of our total sales in that city. The point of the comparisons is to identify the relative proportion of sales in each segment.

In step number three, if there are no data available on industrial sales, then it is necessary to find out if there is a proxy variable for industrial sales which is also current. In the absence of direct information we may have to resort to indirect sources such as establishing derived demand curves for our product. As an example, if we do not have data on the sales of household carpets, we may have to rely on statistics regarding new housing and/or dwelling units built in some recent period. From these data we have to develop surrogate variables and functions to identify the relative portions in each of the market segments with which we are concerned.

If there is no proxy variable for the industry with current sales available, then in step four we will have to look for industry sales available infrequently or even at inappropriate times. Such information, outdated as it may be and not quite relevant to our segments, may present a basis for making adjustments and educated judgments. We may have to select relevant variables representing needed measures (as in the outset of the first step) and correlate them with whatever available industry sales may be available. For example, we may find some figures on industry sales for our area which are outdated by some years. We would have to update it for our purposes and, in the process, correlate the sales series with population growth, employment rates, income distribution or other needed data.

If infrequently collected industry sales are not available, we would use the deductive method to obtain dependent variables such as employment, income, population growth, migration patterns, social attitudes, and other social variables. We then would have to logically and intelligently deduce a relationship between these factors and demand for our products. The deductive method of estimating and forecasting sales potential is only good when complete and timely data are available.

Should independent data not be available, then it is necessary to select weights and measures or factors on logical bases which can be applied to the unaggregated data. Inductive methodology here comes into play because the segments need to be evaluated at the lowest point possible to establish valid relationships. One approach that might be used is to study potential customers and subjectively estimate their buying habits under a variety of conditions. For example, to determine the potential for a resort in a vacation area the following variables might be studied: (1) number of tourists, (2) classification by age, social class, life style, (3) competition in the area, and (4) ease of access to your site.

Thus the basic procedure in constructing sales potentials is to obtain necessary total industry sales and relate them to the performance of a company's segments. In the absence of available timely and relevant data, appropriately constructed data can be used to do the job.

A comparison of the procedures used in inductive forecasting at the segmental level is compared to estimating sales potential:

Inductive Forecasting Process

1. Demand is defined in terms of buying units, number, location, ability, and willingness to buy.

2. Evaluation is made of present accounts for incremental improvement.

3. Calculation of the contribution margin per segment. An effort is also made to determine total contribution by sales call hours to get the contribution per sales call hour.

4. Definition of potential accounts through the use of SIC numbers (or other code) used to define the buying unit.

Estimation of Sales Potential

1. These measures are the starting point of estimating sales potential.

2. Evaluation can be used through contour mapping to evaluate potential accounts. The contour map could compare weak and strong segments as a guide to improvement.

3. Determination is made of the relative proportion in each segment. Contribution can then be determined.

4. Industry sales may be determined with reference to the specific code numbers.

5. Location and evaluation of specific buying units as potential customers through the use of directories such as Dun and Bradstreet (D&B).	5. Computer mapping could be used to locate opportunities.
6. Development of a forecast for segments based on evaluation of present and prospective accounts.	6. Selective opportunities can be identified in each segment by evaluation of the potentials against required effort.

The calculation of sales potential combines elements of both the inductive and deductive approaches. The sales potential method is partially deductive in that it uses industry totals as an aid to evaluate standards. Like the inductive approach, the sales potential method focuses primarily on demand at the segmental level. Sales potential is useful as a standard toward gauging any changes intended to make incremental gain.

MONITORING

At the beginning of this chapter we stressed the need to not only *forecast* but to *monitor*. Otherwise control and replanning will not occur. Reflection on our discussion of forecasting reveals that all the processes noted, especially those that are short term, can and should occur on a real-time continuing basis. Thus, for example, salesmen may be asked to revise their projections monthly or quarterly as needed. Computerized, continuing, disaggregated analysis of actual sales against forecasts can be made daily, weekly, monthly, or quarterly as desired. Similarly, actual costs can be compared with forecast costs using variance analysis to spot significant deviations. The tempo of technological development in each relevant field will dictate the continuity of monitoring needed to anticipate and cope with changes. Monitoring must, of course, include observing each competitor's performance. Hence comparable revenue, cost, and technological information should be generated for each competitor, and the data synthesized and aggregated. This provides a comparative frame of reference needed for full interpretation of company performance.

CHAPTER 5
DEVELOPING A
Marketing
Information System

In previous chapters we have alluded to the diversity of marketing information potentially available. Yet a paradox exists! Those responsible for the marketing effort complain recurrently that they lack sufficient information for the plans, decisions, and actions which they are called upon to make. Kotler puts it this way:

There is too much marketing information of the wrong kind and not enough of the right kind.

Marketing information is so dispersed throughout the company that a great effort is usually necessary to locate simple facts.

Important information is sometimes suppressed by other executives or subordinates, for personal reasons.

Important information often arrives too late to be useful.

Information often arrives in a form that leaves no idea of its accuracy, and there is no one to turn to for confirmation.[1]

There is an evident need for each firm to have a marketing information clearing house which will provide these functions: *collect*, *screen*, *collate*, *analyze*, *store*, *retrieve*, and *disseminate* relevant and needed information. Put another way, "the process of developing timely, pertinent decision data for marketing management can now be character-

[1] Philip Kotler, "A Design for the Firm's Marketing Nerve Center," *Business Horizons*, Fall, 1966, p. 63.

ized more meaningfully . . . as the functioning of a 'marketing information system' rather than simply as 'marketing research.'"[2]

In the small company this may have to be done by the executive responsible for marketing or his staff assistant. In medium-size firms this may be delegated to the marketing research director and his staff. In large firms a marketing information center may be established with a high level staff executive in charge. Kotler, proposes to call this a marketing information analysis center (MIAC). He indicates why he thinks this is necessary:

The marketing information requirements of the modern executive have changed radically in the postwar period while the basic information arrangements have remained essentially the same.

On the one hand, the firm is involved in many more markets and products than ever before, the competitors are able to move more swiftly and deftly; and the environment of surrounding law, technology, economics, and culture is undergoing faster change.[3]

The computer, of course, has made many contributions to ordering and systematizing marketing information. However, in most firms it is grossly underused for this purpose. For example, very few companies use it for simulating various market conditions. Many limit its use in marketing to sales analysis. It is commonplace for a "gap" to exist between executives needing marketing information and those controlling the firm's computer installation. This is due in part to a lack of common language and in part to naîveté on the part of marketing management with regard to the computer applications in marketing.

This is changing. Kaplan indicates that firms find six uses of the computer in marketing in that it "provides better information, assists in decision making, saves time, saves money, helps competitive position, and handles a larger volume of data."[4]

With regard to the firm's marketing information system he observes:

A potential area not mentioned in which computers will be useful to marketers, is in the development of Marketing-Information-Systems (MIS). But to date not much has developed here. Marketers are probably responsible for this lack of advancement, as the capabilities of computers are already sufficient to provide technical back-up required for MIS. In most cases management does not know what information it requires and in what form, or . . . what price it is willing to

---

[2] Richard H. Brien and James E. Stafford, "Marketing Information Systems: A New Dimension for Marketing Research," *Journal of Marketing*, July, 1968, p. 19.

[3] Kotler, op. cit., p. 64.

[4] Robert M. Kaplan, "Computer Applications in Marketing: An Analysis of Corporate Experiences" (unpublished Ph.D. dissertation, Michigan State University, 1968), p. 285.

pay for the data. But, in spite of the human limitations at present, this is an area of great promise for computer use.[5]

The task, then, is to insure that information is available where needed, when needed, by whom needed, and in "input" form so that it helps the user with the best possible plans, decisions, and actions, all things considered. This requires that there be channels established for the flow of marketing information from the outside environment into the firm, upward from those in contact with market members, downward to these same action points, and across at each level within the total organization. As one writer put it:

Rather than mirroring existing procedures, in other words, an information system should be designed to focus on the crucial tasks and decisions made within an organization and to provide the kind of information that the manager needs to perform those tasks and make those decisions.[6]

Kotler suggests that questions such as the following be used to determine marketing information needs:

1. What types of decisions are you regularly called upon to make?
2. What types of information do you need to make these decisions?
3. What types of information do you regularly get?
4. What types of special studies do you periodically request?
5. What types of information would you like to get which you are not now getting?
6. What information would you want daily? weekly? monthly? yearly?
7. What magazines and trade reports would you like to see routed to you on a regular basis?
8. What specific topics would you like to be kept informed of?
9. What types of data analysis programs would you like to see made available?
10. What do you think would be the four most helpful improvements that could be made in the present marketing information system?[7]

Making such an assessment for each action point helps to insure that the staff member will have the information he needs and that he will not be inundated with information of little or no value to him. Additionally, the following benefits should occur with an effective marketing information system:

1. It may provide more information within the time constraints required by

[5] *Ibid.*, p. 294.
[6] William M. Zani, "Blueprint for MIS," *Harvard Business Review*, November–December, Copyright © 1970 by the President and Fellows of Harvard College; all rights reserved.
[7] Kotler, op. cit., p. 70.

the firm. Concomitantly, better performace could be achieved by the entire enterprise.

2. It may permit large and decentralized firms to use the information which is scattered in many places, and integrate it into a meaningful perspective.

3. It may permit fuller exploitation of the marketing concept.

4. It may provide selective retrieval so information-users can be given only what they want and need.

5. It may provide quicker recognition of developing trends.

6. It may permit far better use of material which is ordinarily collected by many firms in the course of their business activities; for example, sales by product, by customer, by region.

7. It may permit better control over the firm's marketing plan; for example, it may raise warning signals when something is amiss in the plan.

8. It may prevent important information from being readily suppressed; for example, indications that a product should be withdrawn.[8]

KINDS AND SOURCES OF MARKETING INFORMATION

Marketing information varies from "hard" data to subjective impressions, from the product of carefully designed research to marketing intelligence, the results of informal observation and inquiry, from facts to opinions. It may relate to the firm's total marketing program or to elements within it. The firm may generate most of it, but it may use outside sources to complement its findings. In many industries, collaborative efforts are made to provide member companies needed information. For example, Associated Equipment Distributors does a periodic census of equipment in use. Various branches of government are additional sources as in the input-output publications of the U.S. Department of Commerce as well as its annual *Industrial Outlook*. The media are another source; for instance, *Sales and Marketing Management* provides two special survey issues each year, one on consumer buying power, the other on industrial buying power.

The sources are about as varied as the information itself. Major potential sources of information include:

1. Feedback from the field sales force.

2. Executive-level observations and inquiries.

[8] Conrad Berenson, "Marketing Information Systems," *Journal of Marketing*, October, 1969, pp. 17–18.

3. Analysis of sales results.
4. Reactions of visitors at trade shows, exhibits, and company display booths at conventions, and at plant visitations.
5. Correspondence from customers including complaints.
6. Feedback on warranties and guarantees.
7. Analysis of competitive advertising and publicity.
8. Spot shopping.
9. Industry news involving the firm's markets.
10. Ideas gleaned from research and development.
11. Observations and suggestions of intermediaries.
12. The corporate legal staff.
13. The advertising agency.

Field Sales Force

Salesmen have a unique opportunity to provide management with a continuing feedback inasmuch as they are in daily contact with customers and prospective customers. Furthermore, unlike marketing research studies, data from this source are generated as occasion provides, from all customer and prospect accounts, not just from a sample of them. This source is invaluable in facilitating short-term prediction of sales and markets. It is an integral part of the field selling job to make a forecast of sales, product by product and account by account. These estimates of likely sales are complemented by an estimate of the share of business being obtained by each competitor. Such forecasts, based on each salesman's observations and inquiries must, of course, be tempered by management judgment and complemented by predictions made through marketing research studies.

The sales force also is in a position to provide management with an early warning system on impending changes in various categories of account. These may include shifts in certain customers' own marketing plans which will influence demand for the company's products, significant changes in personnel in individual accounts, and policy changes that may require strategic accommodation by the firm. In markets characterized by a diversity of technologies, which singly or in combination may influence demand for the company's products and services, salesmen may be the first to know of such breakthroughs.

The sales force can complement staff studies of economic conditions by noting the general state of local business. Finally, inasmuch as the salesmen are in daily competition with salesmen in rival firms, they often learn first about competitive changes, such as the introduction of new products, shifts in promotional strategy, and the relative intensity of the competitor's promotional effort in local markets. The president of one large and successful corporation contends that the role of industrial salesmen as marketing intelligence agents can be greatly improved if:

1. the salesmen specialize in terms of the particular markets they call upon,
2. a formal system for gathering information is created and supported by a built-in process of evaluating and using the information, and
3. rewards—and penalties—reflecting intelligence gathering efforts of the salesmen is built into their compensation plan.[9]

Executive-Level Observations and Inquiries

The sales and marketing executives of the company are those likely to have a chance to provide relevant information, though every member of the management team should be attuned to this responsibility. The firm's purchasing department can be a valuable source of information inasmuch as these staff people are in continuing contact with salesmen who view the firm as a customer or prospect. The purchasing department, in learning who is buying what, can provide inferential findings concerning direct and indirect competitors and perhaps customers as well.

It often happens that executives visiting customers receive information from their fellow executives which might not be shared with the salesmen calling on these accounts. Examples might include the customer's intermediate and long-term plans, impending shifts in policy, and information derived from the customer's marketing research and marketing intelligence. Often, too, such executive contacts turn up bits and pieces of information on developments in the industry in which the customer or prospective customer competes.

Also, since executives are often the representatives of the firm in various trade and industry associations, they derive pertinent information from these contacts.

Analysis of Sales Results

Analysis of sales results may be done either by the marketing research department or by a staff group within the sales organization. It is not strictly research, but rather a continuing tabulation and summary by

---

[9] Reprinted from *Marketing for Sales Executives* with permission of The Research Institute of America, Inc.

product and by territory of sales results as they are received from the field.

Visitors' Reactions

In addition to the sales promotional value of displays and exhibits of the firm's products, they afford an opportunity to glean the reactions of those visiting them. Such inquiries must be brief and uncoercive. They have the advantage of being obtained at the very time the respondent is engaged in analyzing the firm's offering. They may be dealt with either by informal inquiries on the part of those manning the firm's exhibit or they can be self-administering by using short questionnaires to be completed and deposited in a "suggestion box."

Correspondence from Customers

In addition to the public relations value of handling inquiries, comments, and complaints graciously and expeditiously, periodic analysis of the topics customers choose to make the subject of their letters can be an important marketing intelligence input. Complaints obviously must take first priority. These are likely to range over a wide spectrum of matters from alleged deficiencies in the firm's products to its promotional methods, and to the way in which warranties and guarantees are handled. One robin does not make a spring but if numbers of customers make a common complaint it is evident that something must be done. On the positive side this same principle prevails. "Fan mail" on a particular product or product attribute can be inferential evidence that this should be stressed in the firm's promotional efforts.

Feedback on Warranties and Guarantees

Manufacturers and marketers of appliances and equipment covered by warranties and guarantees often take advantage of the return cards to obtain information from the purchaser regarding where the item was purchased, under what circumstances, upon whose recommendation, and for what intended use. It is important that the inquiry be brief and easy to compete lest the respondent feel imposed upon. A large return is insured if the card is required to put the warranty or guarantee in force.

Analysis of Competitive Advertising and Publicity

If the firm is to gain and sustain differential competitive advantage, it must complement marketing research involving competitors with less formal review of competitive advertising and publicity. This involves such matters as noting which trade and industrial media each competitor uses, the key appeals incorporated in the advertising messages, as well as any articles involving competing firms or customers using competing products. Inferences can be drawn in this way about each competitor's media mix, the stress being placed on advertising as a promotional force and, to some extent, the dollars invested.

Spot Shopping

Firms whose products move through various categories of retail outlets often augment the observation and inquiries of the salesmen calling on the outlets by doing periodic spot shopping in such establishments. This provides information on what the retail sales personnel are pushing and what they consider to be the key appeals for not only the firm's products but other competing products that may be stocked. Also, in purchasing competing products and analyzing them, the firm obtains an important input concerning technical properties of the competing goods. Sometimes this is specified as one of the responsibilities of the market research staff. Often, however, it is done by other marketing personnel of the company.

Industry News Involving the Firm's Markets

Procedurally this is almost identical with the way firms monitor competitive advertising and publicity. Here, however, the focus is on the trade press of each industry in which the firm has a marketing stake. Such media are skimmed for ideas that can be incorporated in the firm's marketing effort. The sheer number of such publications warrants delegation of responsibility for monitoring among several members of the marketing staff. It is good practice to encourage the sales force to do this as a by-product of their feedback function.

Research and Development

The prime mission of the research and development group involves *developing new products, refining present products,* and *improving technological efforts* of the enterprise. This group has important contributions to make of a market intelligence kind. For instance, as a by-product of its normal efforts it may happen upon unanticipated properties in the firm's products which can be exploited in the marketing effort. Obviously, too, it is a source of technical information for use in the promotional mix. The marketing group must, of course, translate the "engineeringese" into meaningful want-satisfier language. This group is often called upon to analyze the properties of competing products and, here again, feedback of worth can be provided concerning them.

Observations and Suggestions of Intermediaries

Companies whose goods move through indirect channels often gain valuable information from the channel members. This is particularly important in helping to tailor the firm's product-service mix to meet the expectations of intermediaries and their customers. Where competing products are stocked, inferential information concerning market share can be obtained. Many intermediaries provide services associated with the firm's products and as a result can often make suggestions for technical changes in the line. Also, if a "push-pull" promotional strategy is employed, data regarding demand generated can be obtained.

Corporate Legal Staff

The firm's legal staff, insofar as the marketing function is concerned, deals with such matters as regulatory aspects of government, and protection of the firm's product-service mix by patent and trademark and of certain of its promotional efforts by copyright. As a by-product of such staff work, ideas of worth regarding all aspects of the marketing efforts may be obtained. Also, it can sometimes provide an early warning system on efforts that might not be legally acceptable.

The Advertising Agency

The modern advertising agency might be better described as a marketing services agency. One of its services may be research on pertinent aspects of the firm's promotional efforts.

MODEL OF THE FIRM'S MARKETING INFORMATION SYSTEM

Figure 5.1 depicts the firm's marketing information system. Note that solid and dashed lines have been used to depict information flows which include both line and staff inputs. Solid lines depict flows from line inputs—that is, from observations and inquiries made by other than the marketing research staff. Dashed lines depict flows from marketing research inputs.

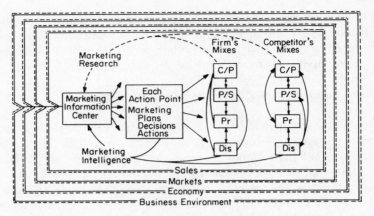

Figure 5.1.   Marketing information system of the firm.

Directing attention to the four outer flows in the figure, both staff and line contribute bits and pieces of information concerning *sales, markets,* the *economy,* and the *business environment.* In the short term, management may rely more on feedback from the field sales force for detailed sales and market data than from marketing research and other sources. In contrast, general intermediate and long-term sales and marketing projections plus economic and environment analysis may be mainly generated by the marketing research staff.

Many sources contribute to the flow of information concerning economic conditons. Considerable reliance is likely to be placed on specialized, secondary sources for intermediate and long-term forecasts. Only very large companies can afford to have their own professional staff of economists.

Environmental factors are so numerous and varied that this flow is likely to be contributed to from multiple sources inside and outside the firm. Included here would be such diverse considerations as governmental regulatory policies and changing life styles of consumers.

In additon to these four categories of information, inputs are needed concerning each of the firm's four mixes singly and in interaction. The mixes, as we refer to them, are

Customer-prospect—the groupings the firm uses to segment its markets based on relevant marketing information.

Product-service—the product and product groups which, in aggregate, comprise the firm's total line.

Promotion—the combination of forces used by the firm to cultivate and sustain demand for its offerings in its several markets.

Distribution—the array of channels through which the firm's products flow to its several markets.

This is shown in Figure 5.1 with both marketing research and marketing intelligence flows occurring. Almost as important is the need for similar flows concerning the four mixes of each competitor (only one competitor is shown in the figure).

There is also likely to be a line flow from each action point as noted in the figure. Only a single action point is depicted, but there are as many of these as there are individuals responsible for marketing plans, decisions, and actions. Inputs occur from each such person.

The person or staff receiving all the flows is shown as the *Marketing Information Center*. This is where the previously mentioned *collecting, screening, collating, analyzing, storing, retrieving,* and *disseminating* take place. Information peculiar to the needs of each action point flows from the Center to the action point. Generally speaking, the firm's organizational channels are followed to accomplish this.

Finally we note that at each point plans, decisions, and actions are occurring affecting each mix singly and the four mixes in interaction. These in turn are monitored, and feedback occurs of a line and staff kind as noted previously.

CRITERIA OF EFFECTIVENESS

What criteria must the marketing information furnished by such a center meet? First, it must be *reliable*. This means that the trustworthiness of both the source and the data have been checked and verified. The user must know the degree of certainty he can place on the information supplied.

Second, it must be *valid* or relevant. This hinges in a major way on the clarity and detail with which the prospective user has stated his needs and the extent to which he has informed the Center of any impending plans, decisions, and actions.

Third, it must be *adequate*—neither too much nor too little. Generally speaking, corporate management is concerned with the "big picture," operating levels of management with specific details. Similarly, long-term trends are important to top executives, whereas short-term projections may be sufficient at lower levels. The critical importance of adequate information at top levels of management cannot be overemphasized. "A lack of information at the operating level may cost the firm some money or time. A lack of information at the top management level may cost the firm its entire existence."[10]

Fourth, it must be *timely*. It is better to have approximate answers when needed than perfect answers when it is too late. The very tempo of business dictates the need for speedy retrieval and deployment of information.

Fifth, it must be *understandable*. An important function of the Center is to convert facts, opinions, and quantitative data into *use* terms. This is particularly important in the case of technical information as well as conclusions derived from sophisticated statistical analysis methods and procedures. To put this in communications terms, it must be receiver-oriented and as noise-free as possible.

Sixth, the value derived must be aligned with *cost*. It is easy to overinform and to do more refined analysis than the use warrants. It is important to remember that the fundamental goal is dual: *to reduce uncertainty* and *to improve quality* of marketing plans, decisions, and actions.

---

[10] Robert L. Johnson and Irwin H. Derwin, "How Intelligent Is Your 'MIS,' " *Business Horizons*, February, 1970, p. 62.

CHAPTER 6

PROGRAMMING THE FIRM'S
Competitive Effort

⌐ Markets, products, and services, like people, come into being, grow, mature, and sooner or later commence to decline. This *life cycle* concept applies to markets, product and service categories, and the firm's own products and services. The usual stages of a life cycle are *initiation* or introduction, *growth, maturity* or saturation, and *decline*. The length of life cycle varies with such factors as: rate of technological change, rate of market acceptance, and ease and rapidity of competitive entry.⌐

GENERAL CONSIDERATIONS

⌐The continuing interaction of product and service segments with market segments underscores the need to consider product and market life cycles in marketing planning and control.⌐

In the broadest, least disaggregated view we might think of markets in terms of sectors of the economy—*private, public, voluntary* (not for profit), or, alternatively, *consumer* and *industrial*. The public and voluntary sectors appear to be growing at a faster rate than the private sector. In combination they now account for about 35 percent of the GNP.

Within each sector are numerous markets—some in a growth stage, some mature, some declining. Some markets extend across sectors—for example, health care, food service, furniture, construction.

Moving in each market are a great variety of goods and services. Some are in the development stage; some are "debugged" with demand growing; some are refined, mass-produced, mass-promoted, and mass-distributed, reflecting a common body of expertise with demand leveled off; some are obsolescent, with demand waning.

Finally, each firm offers an array of products and services in selected markets competing with the offerings of others (Figure 6.1).

The firm must consider its resource limitations in deciding such matters as (1) what products and services to produce, (2) how and where to market them, (3) what share of each market to seek, and (4) in what sectors it will operate. For example, a small firm with limited resources might opt to do business only in the private sector and in selected markets where its offerings do not face major competition. Another, larger firm with relatively similar products and services might decide to do business in all markets where demand exists and in all sectors.

SEGMENT LIFE CYCLE

Life cycle is a useful model for conceptualizing conditions and forces at work in the firm's several markets. It applies equally well to all kinds of segments. However, inasmuch as most companies segment mainly by product, we will use this method as a basis for discussion and analysis.

The product is seen as passing through five phases: *research and development* (prelaunch), *introduction, growth, maturity,* and *decline* (Figure 6.2).

The sales rate is zero in the research and development phase and the profits are negative. As the product is introduced into the market the sales rate begins to pick up but profits may still be negative. However,

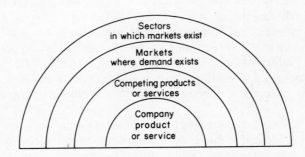

Figure 6.1.   Disaggregation of products and markets.

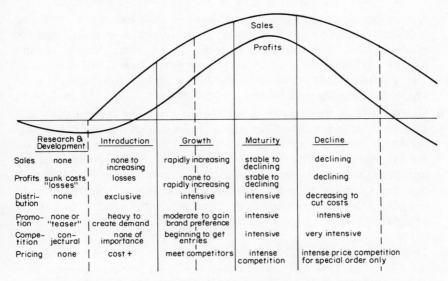

Figure 6.2.   Some characteristics of the product life cycle.

as the segment enters into the growth period, the sales rate increases very rapidly and profits enter into the positive phase. The maturity phase is typified by stable-to-declining sales, and this trend can generally be continued into the declining stage of the segment.

There are several ways in which a marketing manager can determine the state of the life cycle for particular segments:

1. Real-time reports should be available on changes in rates of sales in the segment. Probably the best method of ascertaining the stage of the life cycle with respect to particular segments is keeping track of the changes on rates of sales by segment as they occur and reporting these back to marketing and financial managers for purposes of planning and control. Any change in absolute dollar volume is important. However, it is a good deal more important for the manager to know changes in the rate either up or down as they occur so that he can ascertain rather quickly whether or not there might be changes in the trend and hence a movement into another phase of the segment's life cycle.

2. The length of time in the segment may be compared to whatever the marketing manager considers "normal" for that particular segment. Some companies have been able to compute, based on past experi-

ence, a period of time which they consider "normal" for a particular product's life cycle. For example, some of the soap and detergent products have been characterized as having "normal" lengths of time for the introduction, growth, and maturity phases of the life cycle. These time periods are used by marketing and financial managers as inputs for planning and control.

3. Comparison of the industry's figures may indicate basic trends and may indicate whether or not the company is above or below this particular trend. To some extent, the use of this method depends on the currency of industry figures. However, it is possible in many instances through the use of the SIC to compare company sales with industry sales and to make estimates of a company's segments with respect to the industry's life cycle. This method is a particularly good empirical indicator as it reflects the industry potential sales for the particular segment.

4. The Delphi method can sometimes be used to estimate the stage of the life cycle. This method was discussed in a previous chapter as a method of technological forecasting. Qualified individuals estimate the particular segment's phase in the life cycle. However, the time lag involved in such data collection may negate its use. It is also fairly expensive.

The characteristics of each of the phases of the life cycle will be discussed in this section of the chapter. Considerable emphasis will be given to the financial aspects of this life cycle as they relate to planning of the marketing mix.

Research and Development Stage

The more important characteristics of the research and development stage of the life cycle are suggested in Table 6.1. A basic problem at this stage is a clear definition of which of several alternative products should be pursued with respect to research and development. Both research and development and the marketing segment managers should be involved in the definition of research efforts.

An important consideration here is whether to continue with the product and place it on the market. As accurate a forecast of costs and revenues as possible is needed. It may happen that there are alternative moves to make which show a greater potential return.

A useful categorization of cost classification at this particular stage would be *basic research, new product development, product improve-*

TABLE 6.1   STAGE I—RESEARCH AND DEVELOPMENT

Problems	1.	Clear definition
	2.	Clear description of elements of identifiable costs
	3.	Capitalize or expense
Determination Bases	1.	Individual
	2.	Industry guidelines
Product Evaluation	1.	Importance in terms of usefulness
	2.	Viability in the market place
	3.	What are the expected benefits
	4.	How much will it cost to develop
Cost Classification	1.	Basic research
	2.	New product development
	3.	Product improvement
	4.	Cost and capacity improvement
	5.	Safety, health, and convenience
Cost Characteristics	1.	Incurred with expectation that primary economic benefits will be derived in future periods
	2.	Concerned with improving or developing future benefits for itself
Accounting	1.	Capitalize costs as assets when incurred
	2.	Expense when incurred and charge costs against income
	3.	Capitalize costs selectively
	4.	Accumulate costs until determination made as to whether future benefits exist
Some Budget Considerations	1.	Future receipts less future expenses (discounted to the present) equals future gain
	2.	Use sales to indicate whether to increase or decrease spending
	3.	What is the source of capital
	4.	Capital equipment—what should be used during; what should be done with it after
	5.	Ongoing research; technological changes
Strategy	1.	Examine needs of the market and find means of satisfying it
	2.	Establish market potential through salesmen

ment, cost and *capacity improvement,* and *requirements* for *safety, health,* and *convenience.* These costs are usually incurred with the expectation that the primary economic benefits will be derived in future periods. It should be made clear that while research and development costs might be capitalized and amortized over future periods for purposes of internal analysis, all such costs must be expensed as incurred for external accounting reports. The external accounting treatment may not be realistic but it is a typical manifestation of the accountant's conservatism.

Marketing strategy requires a very close examination of the needs of the market. Individual company and industry guidelines can be used to establish market potentials as a basis for guiding research and development expenditures.

Introductory Phase

In the introductory phase a limited number of models of the product probably should be produced, and particular attention should be given to quality control. The primary areas of concern will be with the creation of demand, funding the costs of introducing the product, selectively attempting to reach an optimum number of segments without spreading too thin, establishing relatively high initial pricing, and experiencing relatively high manufacturing costs. These high manufacturing costs together with the relatively high promotion costs per unit of output will contribute to relatively low contribution per unit in the introductory phase of the product.

From a budgeting point of view, enough funds will have to be committed to give the market an awareness of the product. Therefore, market planning and product development should be very closely coordinated at this stage. The job of selecting the marketing mix with respect to personal selling, advertising expense, and product promotion is the responsibility of the marketing function and segment manager. Hence they should attempt to estimate very closely the variable, programmed, and long-run segment costs and then attempt as closely as possible to coordinate these with the target markets (Table 6.2).

Full-time feedback on the rate of acceptance in the target markets is crucial, and therefore efforts should be made to determine the target contribution by market segments. Particular attention needs to be paid to the rate of change of sales in each of the segments so that rapid changes can be made in the segmental marketing levels to reach changes in the market segments.

TABLE 6.2   STAGE II—INTRODUCTION

Product Evaluation	1.	Limited number of models
	2.	Attention on quality control
Use of Past Life Cycle	1.	Determine time needed to introduce product
Cost Characteristics	1.	Losses anticipated
Some Budget Considerations	1.	Enough funds to create widespread awareness
	2.	Much personal selling—requires extra funds
	3.	Distribution costs increasing High advertising expense if consumer product
	4.	Product giveaways; reduced prices; trade discounts
	5.	Estimate actual fixed costs
	6.	Determine contribution to fixed costs after removing variable costs
Distribution	1.	Limited; exclusive; selective
	2.	Move toward heavy inventory at all levels
Strategy	1.	Promotion
	2.	Use emotive factors
	3.	Strengthen brand preference
	4.	Inform as many market segments as possible

Growth Phase

Special consideration is required in the growth phase to monitor rapid increases in sales as they begin to occur. This means that prime attention is on the rates of change in demand in each of the segments. These rates of change will need to be carefully coordinated with the contribution approach so that cost inputs will be aimed at the target markets which will produce a maximum contribution to profit.

During this period of time there is a need for product differentiation in terms of quality, performance, durability, packaging, and distribution. It is important to establish product differentiation early in the cycle in order to capitalize in the growth of sales throughout the entire length of both the growth phase and the maturity phase.

From a capital funding point of view, a fairly large investment will probably be required in current assets in the form of inventory and receivables. Some capital funding probably will be required for equipment to achieve efficiencies in production. The promotional expense may be relatively high in the initial part of the growth stage; however, the unit cost may become lower as the volume of sales grows in the middle and end of the stage. This particular phase probably will have the highest funding for both expenses and capitalized asset values in the five stages of the life cycle. Therefore, it is particularly important that synchronization occur between the growth of sales volume and available capacity (Table 6.3).

Particularly valuable for this stage are the use of the sales potentials and the matrix approaches recommended in Chapter 4. These techniques can be useful in determining at what point the maximum level of sales will be reached during the maturity stage, and capital commitments can be programmed so that an investment schedule for the future can be developed. It is also important to maintain sufficient price flexibility to quote prices that will meet competition, maximize contribution, and still cover production and distribution costs.

TABLE 6.3   STAGE III—GROWTH

Product Design	1.	Differentiate product in terms of quality, performance, durability, packaging, distribution
Cost Characteristics	1.	Short term
	2.	Heavy emphasis on the contribution approach, particularly to spot rapidly trends by segment-profits or losses
Some Budget Considerations	1.	Promotion expense much lower
	2.	Synchronize available capacity with required capacity
	3.	Highest stage of distribution costs
Strategy	1.	Determine maximum level of sales that will be reached during next stage (maturity)
	2.	Program investment schedule for the future
	3.	Estimate price that covers cost and meets competition
	4.	Improve product and offer services

Maturity Phase

In the mature phase of the segment life cycle, sales tend to become stable. Careful consideration should be given in planning to devote inputs to those segments that will maximize contribution. The emphasis in this stage need not be so much on the rate of change as in the growth stage; however, careful attention should be devoted to those accounts that may be heading for a decline or reduction in sales. Segmental reports on contribution to profit can indicate where promotional inputs—particularly advertising and personal selling—need to be realigned.

The major capital problem to be considered in this stage of the life cycle is whether or not to reinvest capital with the hope that product improvement or differentiation can reinvigorate the sales curve to a new cycle. If differentiation does become possible, it may be possible to extend the life of the product; the increased capital investment could result in a profit contribution for the short run and possibly the long run. If differentiation is not possible, then no capital investment should be made.

Special attention should be paid to the profitable use of assets, particularly in those segments where there is an indication of a decline of sales. A minimum range should be established for acceptable margins in the various segments. Opportunity costs for investment in other segments should be viewed very carefully at this particular stage (Table 6.4).

From a strategy point of view the market segment manager makes decisions as to whether or not to meet the intense competition in this phase of the life cycle. His decision must be made in close coordination with the financial manager with respect to reinvestment considerations and comparative opportunity.

Decline Phase

A very important stage of the life cycle is the decline stage. It is a real art to be able to know when to withdraw a product from the market. Certainly marketing productivity is maximized when we invest capital in segments at stages when they are making maximum contributions to profit. Therefore it is vital to obtain some indicator of the point at which

---

[1] See Theodore Levitt, "Exploit the Product Life Cycle," *Harvard Business Review*, November-December, 1965, pp. 81–94.

we begin to enter the decline of the life cycle. Possible indicators include trends in contribution margin, sales volume, price levels, and comparison of present versus potential use of capital funds (Table 6.5).

The contribution approach can be very useful at this time in indicating those segments that are not profitable. An evaluation can be made by market segment managers whether to discontinue their distribution efforts in these segments, concentrate on the most attractive ones, or simply to milk the profits without investing additional capital.

In the decline stage the market segment manager must have some indicator on a real-time basis of the comparative levels of contribution between segments; he must also have information on rates of change. The establishment of computer routines to develop this information should be made available. The segment manager should work in conjunction with the financial manager to determine whether or not additional capital should be invested and in which particular segments investments should be made.

It is important to have guidelines for either removal of a product from the line or withdrawal from a market. Generally speaking, a timetable and a series of steps are needed lest ill will develop in the affected markets. For example, the first step may occur when contribution drops

TABLE 6.4   STAGE IV—MATURITY

Some Budget Considerations	1.	Much advertising expense
	2.	Depreciation
	3.	Reinvestment considerations (consumer product)
	4.	If differentiation possible and could extend life of the product, increased capital investment would increase in the short and possibly the long run
	5.	If differentiation not possible, no capital investment should be made
	6.	Low return on assets
Cost Characteristics	1.	Distribution costs minimum
	2.	Emphases on contribution approach to spot long-run trends
Strategy	1.	Intense competition—survival of the firm or segment
	2.	Price competition
	3.	Still differentiate

TABLE 6.5 STAGE V—DECLINE

Problems	1.	Determine proper amount of promotional costs to allocate to product
	2.	Determine whether or not to expend research and development funds on product in order to extend effective life or terminate it entirely
Cost Characteristics	1.	If cash flow would be negative in both long and short run, the product should be considered for deletion
	2.	Sales and profits declining
	3.	Costs increasing to stimulate sales
	4.	Consider opportunity costs
Distribution	1.	Appeals made to market segments that are easy to reach (costs reduced)
	2.	Choose one of three: a. continuation b. concentration (most attractive) c. milking

by a given amount below an acceptable level. Direct promotion is curtailed. The second step may be a further drop in contribution and result in limiting sales to stipulated economic order quantities. As contribution fades completely, the final step is taken.

PROMOTION

Programming the promotional effort to achieve the firm's immediate, intermediate, and long-term objectives is a complex task. Promotional effectiveness and efficiency depend in large measure on the specificity and accuracy of the firm's analysis of each of its markets and its products and services interaction in each market. In addition, consideration must be given to what can be achieved by each promotional force singly and in combination. Mention was made earlier of the synergistic effect that can be achieved by a well-planned promotional effort. Finally, marginal analysis thinking must be applied to all promotional expenditures to insure that costs do not exceed revenues. Specifically, short-term promotional outlays to achieve immediate sales must not exceed the contribution from those sales.

In the intermediate and long term, promotional expenditures to invade a new market or to establish a targeted market share in an existing market must not exceed the potential return. In general, each additional incremental increase in market share, beyond a major position in a market, is extremely costly. Here particularly, consideration must be given to the stage in the market life cycle as noted in the previous section. In general, it is more costly to displace competitors than to contribute to total market expansion.

Set forth below is a brief analysis of each promotional mix ingredient. Two questions need to be answered about each one: What is the achievement of each stipulated objective worth? Is there a less costly way of accomplishing it?

Personal Selling

This is the most costly means of promotion. It is difficult to analyze it from a cost standpoint because the sales force performs so many functions in addition to promotion—market intelligence, public relations, representation in trade and industry groups, and, of course, transaction. Further, it can be argued that the salesman's expertise and that of supportive personnel whose efforts he commits are part of what is purchased. Despite these difficulties it is important for management to review what can be achieved through personal selling and then to decide priorities.

In the short term these promotional objectives can be set for selling: focusing, individualizing, and reinforcing the firm's advertising; enhancing satisfaction and minimizing posttransactional dissonance; providing speculative advice and assistance. In the longer term: building ongoing account relations; increasing share of business in each account; providing "image in the flesh" of the firm.

Advertising

Here, too, complications exist in determining effectiveness and attaching costs. Economies of scale may dictate addressing some of the advertising across markets and including in the effort reference to several products. Also, some time lag may exist in gaining promotional impact. Finally, inefficiency is invariably built in by virtue of its mass nature. Rarely does the audience or readership directly coincide with the firm's market or markets.

Short-term objectives may include: inducing immediate purchase; clearing excess or end-of-season inventories; offsetting competitors; and promotional efforts; in the longer term: maintaining the firm and its offerings in continuing awareness; image reinforcement, change, and improvement; sustaining demand where immediate purchase is unlikely.

Sales Promotion Including Direct Mail

Here is encompassed everything the firm does to reinforce its selling and advertising effort. The key difficulty in analyzing effectiveness is that it is complementary to other forces. The exception to this is that sometimes direct mail is used independently as a promotional force. Most often it is short-term in nature though occasionally it is used as a means for maintaining awareness—for example, hand-out catalogs, calendars, and paperweights. Incidentally, the impact of direct mail is easier to measure than most promotional efforts if it is designed to elicit feedback. The most definitive case is where actual purchases occur when this is the sole means of promotion.

Merchandising

This includes all the means used to make the firm's market offering attention-compelling, attractive, memorable, different—logos, packaging, trade marks and trade names, display racks, and so on. Here, too, difficulties in analysis occur. Some merchandising ploys extend across the product line and in all markets, others overlap sales promotion and advertising, others, like selling, provide functions other than promotion alone (e.g., packaging). Short-term merchandising may be used to counter competitive efforts at point-of-sale; longer term it is a prime ingredient of firm and product image. Try to estimate the dollar value of the Coca Cola logo!

Public Relations and Publicity

If this is considered an element of the promotional mix, and the writers think it should be, related expenditures for the most part attach at the corporate level, and, in the case of multilocation enterprises, at the plant or office level. In the short term, two objectives are served: image-building by capitalizing on newsworthy events, and sustaining image by offsetting problems involving community relations. The longer-term objective involves building, improving, and sustaining image.

Pricing

This promotional force is fully as complex as selling and as difficult to analyze. From a short-term tactical standpoint, assuming price elasticity, it may be used to counteract promotional moves of competitors, increase demand, and clear inventories. In a longer-term perspective, price is a symbol of value and hence a key element of product image.

Transaction

Transaction with few exceptions is the responsibility of the sales force. Even in instances where the field salesman has a missionary or detail function, orders mailed or phoned in are received by internal sales personnel. Many factors must be considered to obtain a reasonably accurate estimate of the cost of transactions (see previous example). Some of the more significant positive influences include: size of order, tie-in sales, effective routine, optimization of call frequency relative to account potential, and judicious use of credit and currency of receivables. Negative influences include: special requests, specification of add-ons and modifications of products, excessive commitment of technical advice and assistance, "overcalling," haphazard territory coverage, failure to penetrate accounts in depth, and collection problems.

EFFECTS OF UNFORESEEN COMPETITIVE EFFORTS

In implementing both short-term and longer-term competitive efforts it is important that the individual firm make as accurate an assessment as possible of the promotional plans and actions of its competitors, segment by segment, product by product. Thus in building the segmental forecast and the subsequent promotional program, the individual firm should assess through all legal and ethical means parallel and comprehensive competitive information. In the plans themselves there should sufficient flexibility to allow for unforeseen competitive efforts. This is why each promotional mix ingredient has, as one of its functions, counteracting competition. To do this, flexibility in budgeting (treated in a later section) is absolutely essential.

EXAMPLES OF INCREASING INCREMENTAL PRODUCTIVITY OF A PROMOTIONAL INPUT

The segment manager needs to program his promotional inputs to maximize productivity. This can be done by incrementally improving use of them singly and in combination.

Let us use as a first example a company selling a general line of industrial compressors. Sales effort will be the input used in the example. Sales effort can be measured as sales call hours per account. By comparing the individual performances in a group of salesmen selling to similar segments, the general forms of the relationship between sales call hours and sales can be depicted as in Figure 6.3.

Sales will increase with the number of contact hours. However, diminishing returns will eventually occur as can be seen in Figure 6.3. Note that the productivity curve will become asymptotic and may even turn downward. Given that a salesman expended x_1 hours for y_1 sales and x_2 hours for y_2 sales, a factual relationship between contact hours and sales revenue appears. If total contact hours are increased to x_3, sales would rise to y_3. This information can be placed in the data base and used to develop more precise estimates in the future. Also, the information can be accumulated and used as an instrumental part of the sales-forecasting process.

The objective for each account will be to spend the number of sales call hours that will maximize sales—that is, where $dy/dx = 1$. The same objective would also be sought for each salesman so that the total would be a summation of maximized marginal efforts. Each salesman will be expected to engage in both an appraisal of probability of sales by both present and new accounts and of possible improvements in routing patterns.

A second example of increasing the productivity of a promotional input involves the use of advertising. A mass-promotion chain has a new department introduced experimentally in several stores in two different divisions. After one year of operation a typical department in both divisions showed net segmental losses.

One of the proposals advanced by corporate management was to

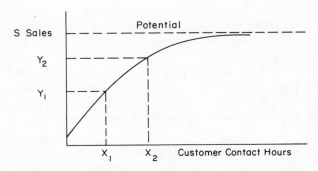

Figure 6.3. Increasing incremental productivity.

increase the advertising. The hope was to increase customer awareness of this department as an integral part of each store in the chain.

Department managers at selected stores in both Divisions A and B were requested to evaluate incremental change at levels of 50-percent and 100-percent increases over existing advertising levels. These estimates, together with those of central management, were used to make the estimated effects shown in Table 6.6.

The incremental effects on sales would be approximately the same in each division: an increase of 50 percent increases sales by 10 to 11 percent; a 100-percent increase in advertising results in 26 to 27 percent more sales.

The decision with respect to productivity is most accurately made in this instance by comparing the effect on net segment margin. An investment of 50 percent more advertising produces $1.33 of added net segment margin in a store in Division A and $2.18 in Division B. An increment of 100 percent produces $1.79 added net segment margin in division A and $3.52 in Divison B. Clearly the best net segment margin is produced by increasing advertising in the stores of Division B.

MEASUREMENT OF MARKETING PRODUCTIVITY

There are usually considered to be three kinds of efficiency: efficiency in use, efficiency of management, and efficiency in marketing technique. Efficiency in use involves judgments on some function solely on its usefulness, regardless of the conditions with which it has to cope. This type is probably most useful for measuring productivity in functional cost centers. Managerial efficiency is used for both long-term and short-term judgments, where the measures may actually show that there are judgments that go in different directions since they postulate different environments. This type of measure may be most useful for measurement of productivity in segmental profit centers. The third is a measure of marketing technique—for example, full-service versus limited-service retail establishments.

The particular type of efficiency question involved would effect the output and input measures to be used. One must specify the unit and what it is that is to be measured, whether it is efficiency in use, managerial efficiency, or a matter of marketing technique.[2]

---

[2] For a good discussion of measures of marketing efficiency see Margaret Hall, John Knapp, and Christopher Winsten, *Distribution in Great Britain and North America* (London: Oxford University Press, 1961), Chapter 4, pp. 33–39.

TABLE 6.6 INCREMENTAL SEGMENTAL EFFECTS OF INCREASED ADVERTISING

	Department in a Typical Store in Division A			Department in a Typical Store in Divison B		
		Projected			Projected	
	Present	50% increase in advertising	100% increase in advertising	Present	50% increase in advertising	100% increase in advertising
Advertising expense	$ 5,315	$ 7,973	$ 10,630	$ 3,766	$ 5,649	$ 7,532
Increase over present year		2,658	5,315		1,883	3,766
Sales increment	217,057	240,000	275,000	258,902	285,000	325,000
Dollars		22,943	57,943		26,098	66,098
% of base		11%	27%		10%	26%
$ of sales per $ of increased advertising		$8.66	$10.90		$13.86	$17.55
Net segment margin increment	($ 18,908)	($ 15,373)	($ 9,380)	($ 4,324)	($ 111)	8,930
Dollars		3,535	9,528		4,113	13,254
% of base		19%	50%		95%	30%
$ of contribution per $ of increased advertising		$1.33	$1.79		$2.18	$3.52

Measuring Output and Input

There are basically three ways of measuring output. The first is the traditional method of using either actual or equivalent physical units. The physical units are weighted on some basis to reflect the relative worth or labor content of the respective units. A second and perhaps more widely used method for measuring total output for individual business units is the concept of value added, in which the sales value of production is measured in constant-dollar terms. The cost of any intermediate materials is subtracted to arrive at value added. The third method is to show sales value of production in constant-dollar terms; this is the method most used by individual companies and is characteristic of the Federal government's published measures of productivity at the industry level.

Problems of input determination are more difficult than those associated with outputs. The ideal input would represent the functional input in the productive process. However, materials are not generally included in the calculation of productivity; they are eliminated if the value added approach is used or else are assumed to have no impact on productivity of final output. There are also problems connected with the combined measurement of capital and labor input. These problems relate to the difficulties associated with defining capital input and to establishing a stock of capital on a meaningful constant dollar basis.

In spite of the difficulties and limitations of data, some efforts have been made to support productivity measurements both in industry and in the Federal government. Many trade associations have been very active in collecting productivity data of member firms. The National Conference Board also publishes figures on productivity. The Bureau of Labor Statistics prepares annually productivity data on over 460 industries by SIC code.

Requirements for Measuring Productivity in Marketing[3]

The first requirement is the ability to measure the overall productivity and unit cost trends of the individual business organization. This can be done through the traditional economic approach. It is also more feasible

---

[3] This section was adapted from a working paper by J. J. Carr, Arthur Anderson and Company, "Concept of Productivity Measurement in Marketing," prepared for the Marketing Productivity Committee, American Marketing Association, May, 1976.

with the use of the contribution approach since the functional costs are assigned to segments as individual inputs to the segments.

The second requirement is a means to measure the real levels of marketing input using the operating cost system proposed in Chapter 3. This information can be made available to the functional cost center managers and to marketing segment managers to control their activities on a real-time basis.

The differences in marketing technique or marketing structure, the third type of efficiency suggested, is slightly more difficult to measure. Two actions are necessary to get this type of efficiency measure. First, the elements of the marketing mix need to be defined and measured in some meaningful fashion. Unfortunately, no comparable physical unit exists that would aggregate all of the marketing components into some meaningful indicator. However, research could provide some basis for marketing inputs for different marketing structures over periods of time.

The second element would be the application of traditional productivity measures to the industry or company to calculate productivity trends over the same markets. This would establish a basis for comparing "real" growth with "real" marketing effort.

TABLE 6.7   WOMEN'S OUTERWEAR VERTICAL PRODUCTIVITY INDEXES—RETAIL SALES PER INDUSTRY EMPLOYEE*

	1958†		1970†	
	Actual	Index	Actual	Index
Total output (million $)	6519.2	100	7307.6	112.1
Input (1000 employees)				
Total	768.1	100	756.1	98.4
Marketing, manufacturers	49.1		54.5	
Marketing, trade	407.7		347.0	
Marketing, total	456.8	100	401.5	87.9
Production	311.3	100	354.6	113.9
Productivity ($1000/employee)				
Total	8.49	100	9.66	113.9
Marketing	14.27	100	18.20	127.5
Production	20.94	100	20.61	98.4

* Source. Robert L. Steiner, "Marketing Productivity in Consumer Goods Industries—A Vertical Perspective," *59th International Marketing Conference of the American Marketing Association,* June 9, 1976, p. 5a.
* SIC Code 233.
† 1970 adjusted to 1958 dollars and female population 14 and over.

The Vertical Industry Productivity Concept

A novel approach to the measurement of productivity in marketing is the vertical industry productivity index proposed by Robert L. Steiner. The vertical industry concept tracks the flow of products past the manufacturing stage through the channels of distribution to household consumers. This concept has considerable virtue in that it emphasizes the total channel rather than comparing institutions on a horizontal basis—that is, retailer with retailer. An example of this type of comparison is presented in Table 6.7, retail sales per industry employee for the women's outerwear industry for the years 1958 and 1970.[4]

Use of the vertical approach emphasizes the channel aspects of distribution. It also enables one to compare the total turnover in the channel, a basic ingredient to the estimation of the stage of a segment's life cycle. The insights from the vertical perspective also have important ramifications for public policy pertaining to the regulation of competition and marketing practices.

---

[4] See Robert L. Steiner, "Marketing Productivity in Consumer Goods Industries—A Vertical Perspective," *59th International Marketing Conference of the American Marketing Association*, June 9, 1976.

CHAPTER 7
PROGRAMMING THE
Physical Distribution Function

The physical distribution function consists of all the functional cost centers that provide the flow of physical supply of goods and services to the market place. Since this is the physical fulfillment of market demand, it is important that those functional combinations are utilized that will give a maximum of customer satisfaction at a minimum of cost to the firm. In order to achieve these goals it is necessary to program the functions for both the short- and long-run market objectives.

SPECIFIC ELEMENTS OF PHYSICAL DISTRIBUTION COST

The specific elements of physical distribution cost discussed here are transportation cost, warehousing cost, order processing cost, and inventory carrying cost. In order to give an idea of comparative amounts, these costs are shown for six firms in Figure 7.1. The amounts vary from a low of $5.20 per hundred dollars of sales to a high of $13.80.

Transportation was the largest of the four costs categories shown. The ranking by firm for transportation cost was: (1) food processing, 65 percent; (2) consumer products, 50 percent; (3) pharmaceuticals, 45 percent; (4) chemicals, 45 percent; (5) machinery, 35 percent; (6) distribution, 10 percent.

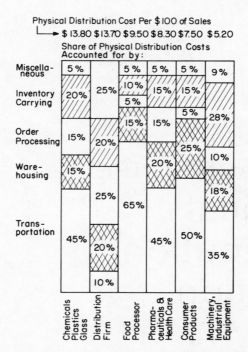

Figure 7.1.   How physical distribution dollars are spent.

Transportation is the purchase and use of intercity carriage such as railroads, trucks, water carriers, airlines, and sometimes pipelines. Competitive rates and routes between these modes must be carefully checked to see if they meet the requirements of the company's marketing policies. Most physical distribution departments have a rate and tariff section whose job it is to check and obtain the rates most favorable to the company's movement requirements.

Some idea of the modal orientation of various kinds of product lines is presented in Table 7.1. Much of raw material and heavy density goods tend to be rail oriented. Manufactured goods tend to be motor-carrier oriented. Much water movement is of bulk and liquid goods easily transferred at terminals. Air-oriented products have special requirements such as those of optical instruments. The diversity of modal orientation and exceptions indicates the need for careful checking of transport alternatives to a firm's markets.

Warehousing costs in the six firms is approximately 20 to 25 percent

TABLE 7.1   ILLUSTRATIONS OF MODALLY ORIENTED PRODUCTS

Rail-Oriented Products	By Rail (%)
Cereal preparations	97.1
Primary copper, smelter products	95.1
Coke and coal briquettes	90.5
Nonferrous metals, primary smelter products	89.9
Animal by-products	75.6
Canned meat	72.3
Lumber and dimensioned stock	70.4
Cigarettes	67.0
Food and kindred products	66.1
Canned specialties	61.3

Motor-Carrier-Oriented Products	Motor Carrier (%)
Cutlery	94.6
Gaskets, all kinds	94.0
Miscellaneous office machinery	93.6
Liquid, dried, or frozen eggs	91.1
Envelopes, except stationery	89.9
Nonferrous metal castings	89.5
Rubber belts and belting	84.5
Special dies	73.2

Water-Oriented Products	By Water (%)
Distillate fuel oil	98.8
Residual fuel oil	97.4
Petroleum and coal products	94.1
Products of petroleum refining	88.8

Air-Oriented Products	By Air (%)
Optical instruments and lenses	42.6
Indicating, recording, and measuring instruments (electric qualities or characteristics)	21.2
Solid-state semiconductor devices	20.5
Test equipment for testing electrical, radio, and communication circuits and motors	13.2
Machine tool accessories, measuring tools, and measuring devices	5.5
Machine tools, metal cutting	5.1
Nonferrous metal castings	4.6
Transportation equipment hardware	3.8
Hoists	3.5

Source: U.S. Census of Transportation.

of physical distribution costs. The purposes of a warehouse[1] are to:

1. Receive and store inbound freight.
2. Select, regroup, and ship outbound freight.
3. Provide inventory records and assist with inventory control.
4. Process shipments such as repackaging or breaking bulk prior to reshipment.
5. Storage in transit.
6. Pool redistribution for shipment to local wholesalers or retailers.
7. Security from natural elements.

The warehousing function can be either private or an integrated part of the company's distribution system or it can be public soliciting business from outside the company. The decision as to which to use depends on two factors—capital commitment and degree of control. If public warehousing is used, costs are largely variable and there are fewer fixed asset commitments. A public warehouse is usually an independent operation with less direct control by the user.

The attachment of warehouse costs to marketing segments is easily accomplished. After the determination of useful segments, the expense and revenue of the warehousing function can be coded and retrieved as desired. Table 7.2 is a presentation of warehouse expense by product group for a public warehouse. The warehouse has two subcenters—handling and storage. Expenses from these two subcenters are attached to product groups to determine segment profitability. Liquor, for example, makes a substantial contribution to profit from storage activity but has a net loss from handling. Tobacco has a profit on storage but a loss on handling. This information can be a basis for better planning and control of warehousing operations.

Ordering costs, the third category of physical-distribution costs, vary widely among the six firms. The range is 5 to 25 percent. This range is easily accounted for by differences in the number of items in the line, frequency of order, size of the order, and required speed of delivery. A brief example in Table 7.3 of parts ordering by the customers of an agricultural implement manufacturer illustrates the differences in ordering costs.

In this company, parts orders are of two types—special orders and regular stock orders. Special orders are executed on the same day and regular stock orders are handled on a routine basis once a month. The

---

[1] Edward Smykay, *Physical Distribution Management* (New York: Macmillan, p. 261).

TABLE 7.2 CONTRIBUTIONS TO PROFIT BY PRODUCT GROUP FOR A PUBLIC WAREHOUSE FOR A ONE-MONTH PERIOD

	Total	Tobacco	Liquor	Food	Hospital Supplies	All Others
Handling revenue	$66,340	$15,874	$19,291	$1,441	$18,833	$10,901
Less: Floor labor	65,359	15,319	20,575	1,083	16,196	12,186
Contract labor	3,050	1,650	200	200	700	300
Handling contribution	(2,069)	(1,095)	(1,484)	158	1,937	(1,585)
Storage revenue	93,685	7,090	29,320	5,973	7,530	43,772
Less: Attachable expenses	64,135	6,653	15,360	2,695	6,030	33,397
Storage contribution	29,550	437	13,960	3,278	1,500	10,375
Segment contribution	27,481	(658)	12,476	3,436	3,437	8,790
Less: Administrative expenditures						
Miscellaneous	500					
Net profit	6,170					

TABLE 7.3   CONTRIBUTIONS TO PROFIT BY TYPE OF PARTS ORDER FOR
AN AGRICULTURAL EQUIPMENT MANUFACTURER

	Special Orders (000)	Regular Stock Orders (000)	Total (000)
Sales	$15,000	32,000	47,000
Discounts	—	1,184	1,184
Warranty	160	340	500
Cost of goods sold	7,098	15,152	22,250
	7,258	16,676	23,934
Gross margin	7,742	15,324	23,066
Variable expenses			
Order processing	760	627	1,387
Prepaid freight	—	650	650
	760	1,277	2,037
Segment contribution to profit	6,982	14,047	21,029
Parts warehouse expense			3,835
General expense			1,447
			5,282
Net profit			15,747
Segment contribution/sales ratio	46.5%	43.9%	33.5%
Orders	158,000	14,400	
Lines	950,000	1,515,000	
Profit per line shipped	$7.35	$9.27	

customer pays for the freight on special orders and receives no discount.
On regular orders the company pays freight charges and also grants a
discount. The special-order business had always been thought to be a
low contributor to profit. After attachable ordering costs were computed
on a segmental basis, it became clear that the percentage contribution of
special orders was greater than that of regular orders. Based on this
information a revision of customer service policies was undertaken with
particular reference to order processing.

Inventory costs are an important fourth category of physical distribution costs, varying from 10 to 28 percent in the six firms. As with other
functional costs, these costs can be inputted to the data base so that
they can be attached to the marketing segment. In Chapter 2 a
discussion was given of the value of including interest cost on an
inventory as a segmental cost. This seems a legitimate attachment since
inventory is produced and sold to particular market segments.

The inventories of the company often must be dispersed geographically in the market place to meet customer requirements. Meeting these needs may require that the company maintain inventory replenishment cycles in the distribution channels which are dictated by the ultimate customer and by competitors' actions. In this sense physical distribution costs must respond to externally imposed effects rather than to internal effects as is the case with production.

Production in many instances has had the option of trade-offs of various kinds relating to labor, alternative machine processes, and timing and sequencing of these alternatives. In most cases in production these alternatives can be decided upon as a result of the internal considerations of the company, subject only to material acquisition. In short, as the product leaves the productive facilities of the company and enters into the physical distribution and marketing channels of the company, there are external effects which are applied on the functional cost centers that tend to determine the ability of the company to exert trade-offs between replenishment cost and customer satisfaction.

Geographic dispersion of inventories in the market place also means that the company usually serves the more distant markets at an increasing unit cost. This is in contrast to the production activity where economies of scale may be obtained based entirely on factors completely within the control of the company. A shipment to points distant from a factory location means higher unit cost of movement than if the products are sold nearby.

The planning and control of physical distribution costs is thus a blend of the desire of the company to minimize its own costs of performing the various functions within physical distribution and yet assuring to the market segments which serve the ultimate customer that the physical distribution cost inputs will result in a maximum of revenue from the customer. Managerial accounting has the mission of aiding operating management to plan and control both functional and segmental operations. This control is achieved by a comparison of the actual costs of a period to a budget which, if properly drawn, is flexible with respect to the level of output achieved. Variations from the budget are then analyzed as to their cause and potential for correction.

The accountant's concern is primarily for control over costs within operating periods. These concerns will mostly be in the short run. The functional manager, particularly in physical distribution, must be concerned with both the short-run and the long-run inputs of costs with respect to their production of revenue in marketing segments. A successful integration of managerial accounting and the physical distribution functions requires that their demands upon organizational design and the chart of accounts be compatible. It is also necessary that they share a common data base adaptable to multiple time horizons. The discussion of these time horizons is arbitrarily divided into short-run and long-run periods of time.

SHORT-RUN PROGRAMMING OF PHYSICAL DISTRIBUTION

The responsibility concept of managerial accounting demands on organization design are sufficiently clear that the costs specifically attaching to responsibility assignments, termed "cost centers," can be collected.[2] No costs are to be included in those of a functional cost center unless the person responsible possesses significant authority over them. As higher organizational levels are reached, it can be said that costs are accumulative and additive. This means that a functional cost center has as its responsibility the sum of costs controllable by the immediate subordinate cost centers plus those costs first controllable at its own level.

To successfully apply planning and control of costs, physical distribution managers must embrace and go beyond responsibility accounting. This is because accounting, while supporting cost minimization within cost centers, does not have any imperatives as to cost interrelationships between them. The cost responsibility requirements of physical distribution are clarified by considering the "trade-off" concept, which allows separable functions to be analyzed within a systems context.

At the first trade-off level, that of component functions, activities and their costs may be altered to effect minimization subject to the constraint that no change may be made independently within a function which would effect a cost trade-off with another function. At the second trade-off level, the constraint is removed and the trade-offs may be made between functions. Changes at the second level must be considered within the context of the entire physical-distribution system by a person with proper comprehensive authority. At the second level, costs at lower levels accumulate and the new costs become specific. Such a person may effect second-level trade-offs subject to the constraint of not changing customer service, since doing so would effect a third-level trade-off between costs and revenue.

Performance reporting for a functional cost center must reflect not

[2] Major portions of this section on short-run programming are adapted with permission from an article by the writers. See also Paul Fischer and Frank Mossman, "The Physical Distribution Management Concept: Partially Fulfilled and in Need of Expansion," *International Journal of Physical Distribution*, February, 1972, pp. 99–102.

only cost within the particular center but also the effects of deviant performance on the costs of other centers. The complete application of the physical-distribution-cost concept to ongoing operations as well as long-range planning is dependent on defining and, if necessary, realigning or establishing cost responsibility assignments.

Concern now turns to the cost methodology necessary to ensure total physical distribution cost control. Such control emphasizes cost minimization in the design of the system and in its performance subsequent to implementation. Cost minimization cannot be absolute but rather must be relative to appropriate levels of customer service. Such service levels may be determined for broad aggregations of the market or may be part of the discretionary marketing mix within smaller market segments.

Cost minimization does not proceed in the manufacturing function without concern for product quality control. Neither can it proceed in physical distribution functions without specification of customer service levels to be achieved. Some firms establish minimum service levels based on competitive influences or the physical characteristics of the products. Where this is the case, cost trade-offs will proceed to the second level—that of trade-offs between component functions subject to their not reducing service beyond the minimal levels.

Other firms may attempt to analyze third-level trade-offs between the incremental costs and incremental review effects of alternative service levels. A study of the revenue effects of alternatives could proceed by a detailed interviewing of customers, especially those with high potential. This might be followed with actual test marketing of alternative customer service packages. Where the risk for cost involved in altering service levels through market testing is too consequential or the reliability of a sample is questioned, testing might be accomplished through computer simulations. All methods are, however, dependent on the firm's ability to measure the differential costs of alternative service levels. This requires detailed knowledge of cost behavior such as that offered by standard costs for physical distribution functions. The third trade-off level is more conceptual than practical until such information is available.

Service levels typically are policy decisions involving large categories of the market and covering extended time periods. However, the availability of behavioral cost data could allow the physical distribution manager to quote the costs of alternative service levels. This would allow the service provided to become a part of the marketing mix. It could become negotiable in such a way as to activate third-level cost trade-offs on a day-to-day basis by those persons closest to the customer.

Cost minimization and trade-off analysis in all functional service areas, including physical distribution, is in vain if the usage of the functional cost is not controlled. Use control can be achieved by envisioning market segments as profit centers. Each market segment manager has his profit responsibility by virtue of dual control of cost and revenue. A wide variety of market cuts can be made, including products, territories, customers, order/shipment size, and channels of distribution. Each cut is made for comparative analytical purposes designed to direct promotional efforts to the profitable segments. These costs may coincide with the responsibility assignments, but may in other cases reflect a mix of responsibility. The prime criterion for an analytical segment is its value as a focal point for customer analysis.

LONG-RUN PHYSICAL DISTRIBUTION PROGRAMMING

The long run is a continuation of many of the problems encountered in the short run. The significance of the long run with respect to physical distribution is that the long-run plans determine the structure within which future physical distribution functions must be performed. Although there are many specific elements that might be considered within the realm of long-run physical distribution planning, three basic areas will be considered: (1) the increasing unit cost of transportation over space, (2) the diseconomies of terminal operation versus the economies of line haul, and (3) trade-offs between the functions of physical distribution at the relevant segmental level.

Increasing Costs of Transportation Over Space

The cost of transporting freight and people over space increases with distance as indicated in Figure 7.2. The unit cost of transportation per mile increases with the number of miles traveled. For example, at one mile the unit cost is 5¢ per mile, 10¢ for two miles, and 15¢ for three miles; this is a constant rate of increase of 5¢ per mile. As the economies of this field begin to operate in the transportation enterprise, this transportation cost may increase at a decreasing rate, in which case the average total unit cost line illustratively would be the dotted line.

Individual firms in an effort to create comparative advantage for themselves over space attempt to minimize the combination of production, transportation, and distribution costs. The calculation of these costs helps to define from a cost point of view a firm's comparative advantage with respect to its competitors. In Figure 7.3 constant average

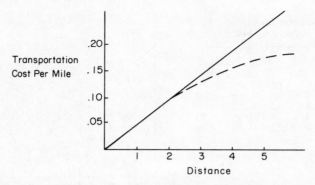

Figure 7.2.   Increasing transport cost over space.

total unit cost of production is assumed to be 10¢ per unit. In other words, for unit 1 the average unit cost of production is 10¢, for the second unit it is the same cost, and so on. This simplistic representation of average production unit costs is in agreement with the idea of charging to the segment only the attachable production costs over which the segment has control. A more sophisticated cost determination might indicate a declining average total unit cost curve. The constant variable costs shown here will be sufficient for our purposes.

The combination of transportation costs and production costs is presented in Figure 7.4 for two firms, firm A and firm B. The two firms are assumed to be spatially separated by four miles. The combined costs of firm A as it moves toward firm B are indicated by the ATUC$_A$ line. The average total unit costs of B as it moves toward A are indicated by the ATUC$_B$ line. These two lines intersect at the mid-point between the physical locations of plants A and plant B. Thus to the left of that mid-point (the mid-point between A and B) firm A has a cost advantage over firm B. To the right of that mid-point firm B has a cost advantage over firm A.

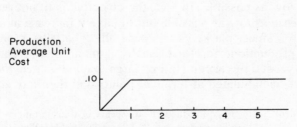

Figure 7.3.   A constant APUC cost curve.

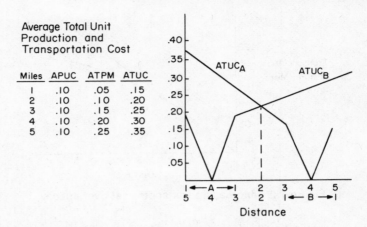

Miles	APUC	ATPM	ATUC
1	.10	.05	.15
2	.10	.10	.20
3	.10	.15	.25
4	.10	.20	.30
5	.10	.25	.35

Figure 7.4.   Intersecting ATUC cost curves.

In a realistic cost-determination situation a firm should have its production, logistics, transportation, and distribution costs figured to the point where it can determine reasonably closely what its cost comparisons are between its own firm and its competitors in particular geographic locations. If a firm has a declining unit cost curve for production, then it may absorb some of the increasing transportation costs as it spreads out over space with the decline in unit cost of production. Theoretically, absorption would be carried on to the point where the increment in transportation over space was equal to the decrement of production cost.[3]

Diseconomies of Terminal Operation versus the Economies of Line-Haul Operations

The charge for moving goods and people over space increases as the distance covered increases. Efforts are made to keep this rate of increase as low as possible. In fact, the objective is to not only keep the rate of increase as low as possible but to have it increase at a decreasing rate. Ideally, since markets are generally spatially separated from sources of production, an effort usually is made to overcome physical distribution costs by accumulating large payloads per move. These payloads are accumulated at terminal points and then moved as volume

[3] For an excellent treatment of the theoretical aspects of transportation costs, logistics, productions costs, and marketing costs, see M. L. Greehut and H. Ohta, *Theory of Spatial Pricing and Market Areas* (Durham, N.C.: Duke University Press, 1975).

shipments to destination markets. The general principle is that the larger the payload or volume per shipment, the greater will be the opportunity of lowering unit costs per movement. Consideration is given next to the diseconomies of terminal operation and the opportunities to accumulate volume moves for lower line-haul cost operation.

Terminals are defined as physical locations or facilities in which the less-than-volume and volume requirements of the movement system are calibrated. These terminal locations are generally of one or more of three types: assembly or consolidation, break-bulk, or combinations of these two. Assembly or consolidation terminals are for the purpose of bringing less-than-volume shipments into larger volume so that capital can be applied to the movement process and thereby lower the overall cost of movement in the physical-distribution system. Break-bulk terminals usually occur on the dispersion side. Some terminals combine both the assembly operation and break-bulk operation in the same physical facility.

Care must be exercised in the use of less-than volume and volume with respect to terminal operations. What may be less-than volume in one type of distribution system might be considered volume in another operation. Volume loads are quite different in a barge with capabilities of payloads of up to 3000 tons per barge load, a rail car capable of handling 100 tons, or a truck that might handle 25 tons. At another level of volume movement, the shopping cart used in a retail supermarket can also be thought of as a volume mover in that goods are picked off the shelf of the supermarket and moved as a volume unit to the checkout counter, thence to the patron's car, and from there to the living unit. The concept of volume and less-than volume is thus relevant to the movement-unit and power-unit combinations that are utilized in the transportation-distribution system to move goods over space.

The definition of the terminal as the calibration point of volume and less-than-volume shipments includes such widely varying facilities as railroad terminal yards, motor carrier terminals, harbor docks, warehouses, grain elevators, and retail shopping facilities. In fact, any place where the calibration of size of shipment occurs is an important part of the distribution system.

Terminal costs are diseconomies in the distribution system in the sense that costs are incurred without movement of the goods across space. One of the characteristics of these diseconomies is that the unit cost curve of handling quantities through the terminal becomes an increasing cost curve as the size of the terminal increases. This requires some explanation. As shown in Figure 7.5, if there are only two points in the terminal, then there is only one cross-move. For example, from

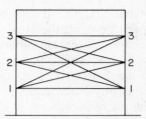

Figure 7.5. Cross moves in a terminal.

point 1 on one side of the terminal to point 1 on the other side there is only one possible cross move. As we add two more points, one more on each side of the terminal, the number of cross-move opportunities jumps to four. As the number of cross moves expands to three on each side of the terminal, the number of cross-move opportunities goes to nine. In other words, as the number of points between which cross-moves may occur increases the number of cross-move opportunities will occur in the ratio ($\frac{1}{2}$ number of points)^2 (Table 7.4). The effect of this on the average total unit cost curve is shown in Figure 7.6 in which the ATUC curve decreases for a short distance but very rapidly turns into an increasing

TABLE 7.4   CROSS-MOVE
PROGRESSION

Number of Points between which Cross Moves May Occur	Number of Cross-Moves ($\frac{1}{2}$ column 1)^2
2	1
4	4
6	9
.	.
.	.
.	.
10	25
.	.
.	.
.	.
20	100
.	.
.	.
.	.
50	625

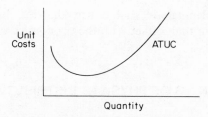

Figure 7.6.   ATUC curve of terminal operations.

unit cost curve. The reason for this is that as the size of the terminal increases, the number of points between which cross movements may occur also increases. Although the number of points increases arithmetically, the number of movement opportunities between these points increases as a greater-than-arithmetic progression. This greater-than-arithmetic increase causes the average total unit cost curve to become an increasing unit cost curve.

The presence of this increasing unit cost curve in terminal operations is important in relating the size and number of terminals to the volume moved in the system. The obvious purpose for accumulating less-than-volume shipments into volume shipments is to be able to experience economies of scale from application of power to the volume moved as the shipment moves across space. These economies of scale can occur in one or more of three ways. First, existing movement units might be loaded more fully toward the capacity of the vehicle; for example, rail cars and trucks might be more fully loaded toward their physical limits than they are at the present time. Second, more movement units might be added to a given power unit, provided it did not exceed the economic or legal limits with respect to such relationships. An example of increased movement units per power unit would be in adding more rail cars to a train load or more barges in a barge train. Third, greater utilization might be obtained from existing movement and power units. For example, efforts might be made to minimize empty back-hauls, or perhaps through better scheduling to obtain better utilization of freight cars, barges, trucks, and accompanying terminal facilities throughout the entire channel.

The effect of these economies of scale on the average total unit cost curve for the line-haul is to create a declining unit cost curve. For example, as more rail cars are added to the train, the cost per car goes down. In the same manner, as heavier payloads are used and greater utilization is made of the equipment, the unit cost also tends to decline. In planning physical-distribution systems, obvious care must be used in the placement of terminals in such a way that the diseconomies of the terminal can be more than offset with the economies of scale in line-haul operation.

STRATEGIC PLANNING OF PHYSICAL DISTRIBUTION SYSTEMS

The programming of physical distribution systems emphasizes the use of trade-off concepts at different functional levels to minimize functional costs and maximize segmental contributions to profit. Perhaps for the first time the data capabilities of a data base as described in the operations chapter (Chapter 3) makes such trade-off analyses possible. The specific uses of these analyses in strategic planning are in such areas as:

1. Determination of proper size for each plant and/or warehouse as defined by sales dollars, weights, and units, and cubed in terms of average and three-foot level over variation of time.
2. Planning the effects of changes in inventory management parameters such as inventory reorder policy, the inventory cycle, transit and safety stock, stock-in policies, and turnovers.
3. Planning the changes in the utilization of commercial and/or private transportation system parameters such as mode utilization, shipping order and reorder policy, new distribution and/or pooling arrangements.
4. Determination of the impact of the operation of distribution points such as break-bulk or pool centers and storage warehouses, and determination of which product groups should be moved through versus inventory.
5. Determination of the impact of various distribution-operating policies on customer service in terms of order cycle time, stock-outs, and back-orders.
6. Determination of the impacts on cost and service or changes in production cycle or schedule time or changes in the vendor's lead time.
7. Determination of the impacts of costs and service changes in customer mix, order size, and/or seasonal patterns.

The relationship between the physical system planning and control management is the starting point for such analysis as the market segment at the lowest delivery echelon normally used by customers. The component elements of physical systems must be related in a relevant manner to the alternative segmental combinations of products, customers, territories, order/shipment size, and/or channels of distribution.

TECHNIQUES FOR STRATEGIC PLANNING

The techniques for strategic planning of physical distribution systems have been classified by Donald Bowersox as symbolic representation, analytic, and simulation. Each technique is evaluated in Table 7.5 with respect to certain attributes.

The symbolic replications of comparative and break-even analyses are generally analytical but have no other attribute; break-even analysis can be used to establish relationships. These three techniques are often used in combination to supplement each other.

The analytic techniques generally have an objective function which is to be either maximized or minimized. The two general classes of analytic techniques are gravity-flow and linear-programming models.

Gravity-flow-location models usually select an optimum location such as a plant, warehouse, or retail store location. Other gravity-flow models can be used to supplement the gravity-location model.

Probably the most popular of the analytic techniques is the wide range of linear-programming models. These all aim at specifying a network of optimal paths under a set of expressed constraint conditions. The most widely used are the transportation and simplex models. The other types are more complex and are capable of handling more sophisticated problems.[4]

To some extent linear-programming techniques can be viewed as treating an entire physical distribution system. These programs are good for the purposes for which they are designed, but users should not try to exceed the capacity of the technique.

Sensitivity analysis can be done with linear programming. New sets of parameters can be inputted into a network and the effect of the change calculated for the system. This can be valuable for asking certain types of "what if" questions.

A severe drawback of linear programming is that it is not dynamic— that is, time is not a variable in the problem. Nor can there be more than

[4] For a more detailed discussion of these methods see Donald J. Bowersox, *Logistical Management,* second edition (New York: Macmillan, 1978). Also see Frank Mossman, Paul Bankit, and O. Keith Helferich, *Logistics Systems Analysis* (Washington, D.C.: University Press of America, 1977).

TABLE 7.5 CLASSIFICATION OF STRATEGIC PLANNING TECHNIQUES IN TERMS OF SIX SELECTED ATTRIBUTES OF IMPORTANCE TO REQUIREMENT EVALUATION

Category of Planning Technique	Technique Attribute					
	Analytic	Dynamic	Echeloned	System	Requires Computer**	Adaptable to Sensitivity Analysis
Symbolic replications						
Comparative analysis	Yes	No	No	No	No	No
Break-even analysis	Yes	No	No	No	No	Yes
Flowcharting	No	No	Yes	No	No	No
Analytic techniques						
Gravity location	Yes	No	No	No	No	No
Transportation LP*	Yes	No	No	Partial‡	No	Yes
Simplex LP	Yes	No	No	Partial	Yes	Yes
Mixed integer LP	Yes	No	No	Partial	Yes	Yes
Separable LP	Yes	No	No	Partial	Yes	Yes
Transshipment LP	Yes	No	Yes	Partial	Yes	Yes
Decomposition LP	Yes	No	No†	Partial	Yes	Yes
Variable Range LP	Yes	No	No	Partial	Yes	Yes
Simulation techniques						
Static	No	No	Yes	Partial	Yes	Yes
Dynamic	No	Yes	Yes	Yes	Yes	Yes

Source. From *Logistical Management*, second edition, by Donald J. Bowersox. By permission of Macmillan Publishing Co., Inc. Copyright © by Donald J. Bowersox.

* LP: linear programming.

† Advanced applications of decomposition linear programming do provide the capability of dealing with three echelons in the design solution.

‡ These techniques (partial) are total-system in terms of the number of echelons modeled, with the exception that inventory level must be determined based on a calculation.

** In a technical sense, all of the techniques can be utilized on a manual basis. The classification is in terms of logistical strategic planning and practicality of application.

118

one stage in the problem. The solution is good only for the time period or problem stage as formulated.

Simulation techniques of all types are increasingly being used to design physical distribution systems. The need to show functional flows between component parts of a system has led to the use of simulation models. The models are either static—that is, non-time-dependent—or dynamic, which allows the model to treat time and/or sequential stages of a problem in an interrelated manner.

The value of these tools is that they can be used to plan both simple and complex physical distribution systems which will effectively minimize total functional costs and maximize contribution to profit. The models assume the availability of the proper data. The data base as discussed in Chapter 3 assures that the data can be made available in usable forms and time frames. Therefore, the physical distribution systems planner is now able to fully use his analytical skills in combination with all relevant parts of the company and the markets it serves.

CHAPTER 8
BUDGETING FOR
Operational
Planning
AND
Control

Marketing management has the responsibility to make sound and prudent use of the firm's financial resources in achieving marketing objectives. To facilitate this financial planning and control, budgets are constructed containing both revenues and expenditures. The marketing budget, once formulated, is a means of measuring and controlling the implementation of marketing plans.

GENERAL MARKETING BUDGET CONSIDERATIONS

There are several criteria that need to be met in the preparation of a marketing budget:

1. The budget should be prepared in such a way that it is congruent with the firm's financial objectives, fiscal policies, available monetary resources, and likely marketing opportunities.
2. The necessary supportive data on projected costs and revenues should be included.

3. There should be provision for contribution centers by market segments.
4. Frequent checking and replanning needs to be done because of the numerous uncontrollable factors that can affect marketing. Sufficient flexibility must be allowed to permit tactical accommodation on the part of the firm to changing market factors.
5. The budget must be so planned and administered that cost/revenue information is easily deployed to the numerous action points within the organization.

The preparation of the budget normally starts with a constructively critical review of the firm's past budgeting experience. The projection of revenues into the forthcoming period rests on the firm's tactical view of the price and quantity of each item that will be sold in each of the firm's markets. This projection of revenue becomes the basis for projecting both functional and segmental costs that will be incurred to produce the forecasted revenues.

Checkpoints need to be established for reviewing actual performance against the projections. This integral part of budgeting assures that both control and replanning occur. Any variances in costs or revenues are noted and become the basis for management replanning at relevant decision and action points.

For a marketing-oriented firm, sales segments become the basic analytic units for profit optimization. They are the focal point for measuring the interaction of promotional efforts and contribution. A general analytic model will be developed based on the residual contribution theory developed in Chapter 2. The budget model will be used to analyze alternative plans and to quantify the final plan into the segment budget. The budget model will also become a control tool as it is used to measure actual segment performance. Stated properly, the budget is flexible and can be used to find allowable expenses for the actual sales volume resulting in a period.

BASIC BUDGET MODEL

The basic budget model for sales segments is a multiple regression formulation incorporating product- and customer-related variables and constants representing attachable fixed costs. The model to be developed is expressed as:

Segment contribution $= c_1 x_1 + c_2 x_2 + c_3 x_3 - e_1 y_1 - e_2 y_2 - FC - PC$

where

c_{1-3} is the contribution per unit of product. The contribution of a product unit is its revenue per unit less all product-related variable costs. These variable costs always include variable production costs but may also include inventory holding costs and transportation costs where such costs are a function of units sold.

x_{1-3} represents product unit sales. Where a particular product line segment is being analyzed, only one product unit variable may be needed. Where customer segments are being analyzed, the product unit variables may become extensive.

e_{1-2} represents variable expenses which behave as a function of a variable other than product units. Typically there will be physical-distribution costs that vary according to customer-related variabilities such as ton-miles shipped or invoices processed.

y_{1-2} are non-product-related factors of variability such as the ton-miles shipped or invoices processed. It is the measure of activity to which the non-product-related costs vary.

FC denotes specific fixed costs attachable to the segment being analyzed. This term excludes promotional costs but does include specific production and physical-distribution costs.

PC denotes promotional costs to be used to secure the segment contribution. These costs include advertising, general promotion, and direct selling costs. PC may be expanded to include a variable cost element where, for example, sales commissions are paid as a function of sales volume.

There are two features of the model that require additional comment. First, this is a residual income type model which means that cost-of-capital charges are levied against the segment. Those cost-of-capital charges that are variable are included as variable costs. For example, inventory holding costs include a cost of capital charge; typically this cost is product-related and is deducted from the revenue of a unit to arrive at the contribution of a unit of product. Other variable cost-of-capital charges may be customer-related rather than product-related. For example, the cost of carrying receivables is a function of the customer's payment pattern. Remaining cost-of-capital charges, such as those resulting from the investment in fixed assets, are fixed in nature and are included in the fixed costs attached to the segment.

A second major concern of the model is the segregation of promotion costs. Since these costs are either variable or fixed in nature, it might appear that they could be included and commingled with the three other cost categories preceding them in the model. This is not desirable, however, from a planning perspective. Promotion costs should be considered the ammunition and at least partial cause of sales. Thus it is desirable to test the results of various levels of promotion costs. This means that promotion costs become a type of specified independent variable, while all other costs are dependent variables resulting from the sales volume estimated to correspond with a given level of promotional effort. Clearly, the planning use of the model would be impaired by not segregating the promotional cost component. In particular, it should be noted that sales commissions are often deducted from the revenue of a unit to arrive at its contribution. This is not desirable because it assumes that the commission is an inescapable product-related cost. This is not true since alternative promotion methods could be used and, in fact, should be considered. Thus, since salesmen's compensation is a relevant part of the promotion mix, it should be included in the ammunition, or *PC*, cost component.

Hierarchy of Segment Analysis

The general model developed above is applicable to any level of analysis ranging from the analysis of a single customer to the analysis of a sales territory, product line, or entire division. However, the includable components increase as one proceeds to more aggregated levels of analysis. The product unit contribution variable is applicable to all levels of analysis, since all segments reflect some aggregation of product unit sales. Generally speaking, remaining non-product-unit variable costs tend to be customer-related and are also calculable at all levels of analysis. An exception might include transportation costs incurred jointly for several customers such that the transportation cost could not be included in the analysis of a single customer but could be included in an analysis of the sales territory in which the given customer is located.

Fixed costs become increasingly attachable as one proceeds to higher levels of analysis. For example, there are probably no fixed costs that would attach exclusively to sales to a given customer. Likewise the fixed cost of maintaining a warehouse would not be specific to any one sales territory but would be specific to a sales district, made up of several territories which it serves. Similarly, the fixed cost of production machinery used exclusively for one product would not attach to any customer or product analysis that did not include all units sold of the product.

Special concern must be given to specific promotional costs. As is true with fixed costs, more promotional costs become attachable as one proceeds to higher levels of aggregation. However, as alternative levels of promotional efforts are considered for a given segment, the estimated results of the specific efforts must be considered in light of other promotional efforts which, though not specific to the segment, do effect its performance. For example, national advertising of a product is probably not attachable to the territory of a given salesman. Yet the results of specific efforts within the territory are due to the interactive and perhaps synergistic effects of the specific efforts and the national advertising.

Information Requirements

The model for segmental analysis achieves its full potential when it is linked to a modular data base which quickly and precisely supplies required contribution, variable cost, and specific fixed cost components. To use the modular data base, the alternative sales plan must specify, in addition to the level of promotional expenditure, the following information:

1. Sales projection in units; this allows the modular data base to project the contribution of the units sold by deducting product-related variable costs from the projected sales price of the units.
2. Estimate of the use of non-product-related factors of cost variability. This allows variable customer-related costs to be estimated. For example, the sales projection would specify what amount of sales would be made to given customers so that the accounts receivable, carrying cost, and transportation costs could be estimated. It is essential that estimates be made in units of measurement consistent with those used by the modular data base; the estimates should reflect the sensitivity of the segment's net margin to alternative usages of these variable costs.
3. A precise description of the segment being analyzed which is consistent with the fixed-cost attachment levels contained in the modular data base. This assures a simple attachment of relevant fixed costs to the segment.

The above information must also be supplied for actual sales results of a segment so that the budget may be applied to actual results to measure deviations in performance. The use of the budget model for variance analysis will be discussed in a subsequent section of this chapter.

Example of Applying the Model

Let us use a sales district as an example. Assume that three products are sold in the district and that the modular data base contains cost elements applicable to the district (Table 8.1).

The data Table 8.1 assume that the transportation cost is the same per ton-mile for all units shipped. The data also assumes that the receivable holding costs and order processing costs cannot be meaningfully isolated by product or customer attributes. The order-processing cost includes all paperwork resulting from customer sales defined in terms of the time taken to prepare an invoice. Thus the invoice equivalent becomes the measuring unit for paperwork costs caused by sales.

Analysis of a Market Plan

Marketing management wishes to test the likely financial results of the following promotional efforts: (1) advertising, $40,000; (2) promotions, $15,000; (3) salesmen's salary and travel, $60,000; and (4) sales commis-

TABLE 8.1   BASIC BUDGET MODEL

	x_1	x_2	x_3
Product unit related			
Product			
Revenue per unit	$40.00	$50.00	$25.00
Standard variable production cost per unit	20.00	28.00	13.00
Inventory holding cost (3% of variable cost, 1 month holding period)	.60	.84	.39
Inventory handling	2.00	1.16	.61
Contribution per unit	$17.40	$20.00	$11.00

Other variable costs
Transportation, $.80 per ton-mile
Receivable holding cost, 1 month average payment period at a cost of capital charge of 18% annual rate or .015 revenue.
Order processing cost, $1.20 per invoice equivalent

Specific fixed costs
Fixed cost of district office:

Short run, controllable	$18,000
Long run, noncontrollable	12,000
Total	$30,000

sions, 4 percent of sales. As a result of these efforts it is projected that:

1. Sales will be 10,000 units of x_1, 6000 units of x_2, and 4000 units of x_3.
2. 80,000 ton-miles of shipping costs will be required.
3. 1800 invoice equivalents of paperwork will be required.

According to this projection, total sales revenue would be computed as follows:

$$
\begin{array}{lr}
10{,}000\,x_1 \times \$40 = & \$400{,}000 \\
6{,}000\,x_2 \times\ \ 50 = & 300{,}000 \\
4{,}000\,x_3 \times\ \ 25 = & 100{,}000 \\
\hline
\text{Total} & \$800{,}000
\end{array}
$$

The anticipated net segment contribution of the plan would be estimated using the general budget formula as follows:

Net segment contribution = $\$17.40\,x_1$ + $\$20.00\,x_2$ + $\$11.00\,x_3$
− $.80 ton-miles − $1.20
invoice equiv. − $.015 revenue −
$30,000 fixed district cost −
$115,000 fixed promotion cost −
$.04 revenue

Inserting the values of the variables:

Segment contribution = $17.40 × 10,000 + $20.00 × 6,000 +
$11.00 × 4,000 − $.80 × 80,000 −
$1.20 × 1,800 − .015 × $800,000 −
$30,000 − $115,000 − .04 × $800,000
= $174,000 + $120,000 + $44,000 −
$64,000 − $2,160 − $12,000 −
$30,000 − $115,000 − $32,000
= $82,840

Alternative sales projections may be tested by repeated applications of the general formula. The above projections are incorporated into the final segment budget shown in Table 8.2. The statement follows the residual contribution format developed in Chapter 2.

TABLE 8.2   BUDGETED PERFORMANCE: DISTRICT A (RESIDUAL INCOME APPROACH)

Revenue		
10,000 x_1 × $40	$400,000	
6,000 x_2 × 50	300,000	
4,000 x_3 × 25	100,000	$800,000
Less variable product related costs		
10,000 x_1 × $22.60	$226,000	
6,000 x_2 × 30.00	180,000	
4,000 x_3 × 14.00	56,000	462,000
Product contribution margin		338,000
Less variable physical distribution and promotion costs		
Transportation, 80,000 ton-miles × $.80	$64,000	
Invoice costs, 1,800 invoice equiv. × $1.20	2,160	
Receivable carrying cost, .015 × $800,000 revenue	12,000	
Sales commissions, .04 × $800,000 revenue	32,000	110,160
District contribution margin		227,840
Less short-run controllable fixed costs		
District office	$18,000	
Advertising	40,000	
Promotion	15,000	
Salesmen's salary and travel	60,000	133,000
Segment controllable margin		94,840
Less long-run noncontrollable costs		12,000
Net segment margin		$82,840

Applying Basic Cost-Profit-Volume Analysis

Cost-profit-volume analysis is built on the premise of only one aggregated variable cost component which behaves as a function of revenue.

In order to convert the general segment model into the cost-profit-volume format, one must first express all variable costs in the segment as a function of revenue as follows:

Total Variable Costs	
Product x_1, 10,000 × $22.60	$226,000
Product x_2, 6,000 × $30.	180,000

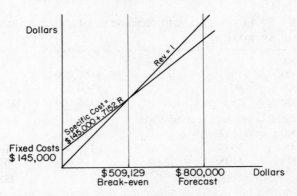

Figure 8.1.   Cost-profit-volume analysis for a market segment.

Product x_3, 4,000 × $14.	56,000
Transportation $.80 × 80,000	64,000
Paperwork $1.20 × 1,800	2,160
Accounts receivable .015 × $800,000	12,000
Sales commissions .04 × $800,000	32,000
Total	$572,160
Total variable cost ÷ revenue of $800,000	.7152

Thus the cost-profit-volume equation would be stated:

$$\text{Segment contribution} = \text{Revenue} - .7152 \text{ revenue}$$
$$- \$145,000 \text{ fixed costs}$$

Graphically it would appear as shown in Figure 8.1. The graph computes a break-even point of $509,129; stated another way, sales could fall 36 percent before the segment fails to justify its existence.

The simplification of the model into the traditional cost-profit-volume format is dangerous since by necessity a constant mix of products and a constant ratio of non-product-related variable costs is assumed to prevail at all volumes. Since this is not a realistic assumption, the simple cost-profit-volume model is limited in usefulness and should be used only to make a rough estimation of the effect on segment margin of an overall volume change where it may be reasoned that the product and service mix will not materially change.

OPTIMIZING SEGMENT CONTRIBUTIONS

At each level of segment aggregation, it is the responsibility of management of that level to see that the underlying market segments make a sufficient contribution to cover the specific fixed costs of that level. In addition there should be an adequate excess of the contribution over specific fixed costs to contribute to the remaining nonspecific fixed costs and to the firm's profit. For example, a district manager must attempt to see that the underlying sales territories bring forth sufficient contribution to cover the specific fixed costs of the district and to make a reasonable contribution to remaining corporate costs and profits. At the level of the firm, all costs become specific, and aggregated contributions will hopefully cover them and produce a profit. If, at any level, contributions of constituent segments are inadequate in terms of either profit goals or the segment's potential, the operating budget of the segment must be reformulated to more closely align with the firm's goals.

In reality, one cannot proceed to budget a firm's operations without recognizing the constraints upon the firm. Typically, the extent of promotional expenditures is limited by available funds and/or management time. If there were no constraints one would proceed to make promotional expenditures in each segment until the marginal contribution of the last dollar of expenditure equalled one. Where, however, funds are limited, the goal becomes one of equating the marginal contribution of the last dollar spent in each segment such that no shift of effort would increase total profit. However, it is not realistic to measure the marginal contribution of a dollar of promotional expenditure. Instead, one must settle for rough incremental measures of contribution versus expenditure. Insight into the effectiveness of promotional efforts across segments might be obtained by measuring incremental contribution versus incremental promotional expenditures by segment as follows:

Sales Territory	1	2	3
Increase in contribution, 1977 vs. 1976	$50,000	$30,000	$45,000
Increase in promotional expenses, 1977 vs. 1976	30,000	10,000	20,000
Incremental indicator	1.67	3	2.25

The above indicators should lead to a study as to the cause of the difference of the results and, unless the difference is caused by external intervening factors, would lead to a shift of efforts into territory 2. In order to encourage only the more potentially profitable increases in promotional efforts, corporate management might specify a minimum incremental indicator which must be met in order for a segment to receive added funding.

The incremental indicator may also be used to analyze adjustments to a segment's initial budget. For example, suppose that the segment having the previously developed budget formula saw the following opportunity: It is forecast that if $5,000 were spent on advertising the superior nature of product x_2, 2000 added units would be sold; however, 1000 fewer units of x_1 would be sold. The change in segment sales would add 2000 more ton-miles of transportation and 100 added invoice equivalents. Without reworking the entire equation, the opportunity could be evaluated as follows:

Incremental contribution:	
2000 units of x_2 × $20	$40,000
Less:	
1000 units of x_1 × $17.40	(17,400)
2000 ton-miles × $.80	(1,600)
100 invoice equivalents × $1.20	(120)
Accounts receivable $60,000 increase in revenue × .015	(900)
Increase in commissions, $60,000 increase in revenue × .04	(2,400)
Incremental contribution	$17,580
Incremental promotional cost	5,000
Incremental indicator, $17,580 ÷ $5,000 =	$3.52

A second type of constraint to be considered is the scarcity of capacity required to build or distribute the product. In theory such a problem is dealt with using linear-programming techniques at the corporate level. Strict adherence to linear-programming concepts will maximize the contribution of scarce resources but it also requires centralized decision-making. Several alternatives are available where decentralized decision-making is desired. A popular approach is to charge for the use of scarce resources at a value approximating their anticipated contribution to profits. In this way, what would otherwise be a fixed cost becomes a variable cost for planning purposes. No segment will use the capacity unless it can pay the cost which means that the segment is earning more per unit of time of scarce resource than is required. Another alternative is to have segments compute their contribution per unit of use of the scarce resource and to allocate the resource to those segments producing the largest return.

CONTROL THROUGH VARIANCE ANALYSIS

Variance analysis compares actual results of a segment to the original budget. The total variance in contribution is broken down into subvariances which explain the causes of a difference between actual and planned performance. This is done in order to spot a need for corrective action and/or to improve future planning. Prior to discussing means by which variances may be analyzed, two concepts must be emphasized. First, the analysis of sales performance by a segment should not be confused by cost variances resulting from the production of the units sold or the provision of physical-distribution services used. Such variances are the responsibility of the functional cost centers providing goods and services to sales segments. The management of selling segments are given standard costs to use in decision-making, and thus standard costs must be used in measuring performance. Secondly, it must be realized that not all variances calculated for a segment are the responsibility of the segment's management. For example, a change in selling price will cause a variance for the segment even though it was ordered by a higher level of management. Thus the segment becomes an analytic unit for planning purposes and as such may reflect multiple responsibilities.

The analysis of actual versus budgeted performance may be broken down into three major components: an analysis of sales performance, analysis of nonproduction costs specific to the segment, and an analysis of incremental promotional productivity. Table 8.3 is an analysis of sales performance which focuses on the difference between the actual and budgeted product-contribution margin. The exhibit is based on total unit sales of 21,000, broken down as follows:

$$
\begin{array}{ll}
11{,}000\ x_1\ \text{at}\ \$38 & \$418{,}000 \\
4{,}500\ x_2\ \text{at}\ \$50 & 225{,}000 \\
5{,}500\ x_3\ \text{at}\ \$23 & \underline{126{,}500} \\
\text{Total} & \underline{\$769{,}500}
\end{array}
$$

Analysis begins by determining the deviation from budget caused by the actual sales price per unit. Actual versus budgeted price is analyzed at the actual level of sales for each product. The fact that products x_1 and x_3 were sold at a price below that budgeted reduced the district's contribution by \$33,000. Attention is then directed to the product-mix composition of the 21,000 units actually sold. The change in district contribution caused by selling a larger proportion of x_1 and x_3 at the expense of x_2 reduces the district contribution by \$13,000. The net mix variance is always zero as to units; the dollar discrepancy is caused by the trade-off of units with differing unit-contribution margins. The mix variance is easily calculated by comparing the actual sales of each unit with the unit sales that would have resulted had the total volume of 21,000 units been sold in the budgeted 50/30/20 mix. Since the sales price

TABLE 8.3   BUDGETED VERSUS ACTUAL SALES PERFORMANCE: DISTRICT A

Analysis of Product Contribution

Actual product-contribution margin $308,900

Variance due to sales price

Product	Actual Price	Budget Price	Variance	Units Sold	Total
x_1	$38	$40	$2 U*	11,000	$22,000 U
x_2	50	50	—	4,500	—
x_3	23	25	2 U	5,500	11,000 U
					33,000 U

Variance due to mix:

Product	Actual Units	Actual Volume at Budget Mix	Variance	Standard Contribution per Unit	Total
x_1	11,000	10,500 (50%)	500 F†	$17.40	$8,700 F
x_2	4,500	6,300 (30%)	1800 U	20.00	36,000 U
x_3	5,500	4,200 (20%)	1300 F	11.00	14,300 F
Total	21,000	21,000	-0-		13,000 U

Variance due to volume:
21,000 units actual versus 20,000 budgeted equals 1000 units favorable in standard mix:

Product	Unit	Contribution Per Unit	Total
x_1	500 (50%)	$17.40	$8,700
x_2	300 (30%)	20.00	6,000
x_3	200 (20%)	11.00	2,200
			16,900 F

Budgeted product-contribution margin $338,000

* U; unfavorable.
† F: favorable.

variance has already been isolated, the mix variance, in dollars, is computed using the budgeted sales price.

The final sales variance is a comparison of the actual versus budgeted total sales volume. Table 8.3 shows that 1000 units in excess of the budget were sold. Since variances due to sales price and mix have already been analyzed as they apply to actual volume, the contribution due to volume is quantified using the budgeted price and the budgeted 50/30/20 mix. The three sales variances explain the difference between actual and budgeted product contribution. It should be noted that all

TABLE 8.4   ANALYSIS OF DISTRICT A PERFORMANCE AT ACTUAL SALES LEVEL

	Actual Results	Budget for Actual Sales Level	Cost Variances
Actual product contribution	$308,900	$308,900	
Less variable costs			
Transportation ($.80/ ton-mile)	94000/$75,200	91,000/$72,800	$2400U*
Invoice cost ($1.20/ invoice equiv.)	1820/ 2,184	1,850/ 2,220	36F†
Receivable cost (.015 × revenue)	13,000	$769,500/$11,543	1457U
Sales commissions (.04 × revenue)	10,560	$769,500/$10,560	—
District contribution margin	207,956	211,777	3821U
Less short-run controllable fixed costs			
District office	$18,780	$18,000	780U
Advertising	35,000	40,000	5000F
Promotion	15,000	15,000	—
Salesmen's salary and travel	58,000	60,000	2000F
Segment controllable margin	$81,176	$78,777	2399F
Less long-run, noncontrollable fixed costs			
District office	12,000	12,000	—
Net segment margin	$69,176	$68,777	$2399F

* U: unfavorable.
† F: favorable.

analyses are made using the standard product cost. Any variance between actual and standard product costs are isolated in the production cost center responsible for the variance, and the analysis of sales performance is not confused by their inclusion.

The next major component of performance analysis compared the costs incurred for and/or by the segment in order to produce and service the actual sales volume. In essence, the segment is studied to determine whether the nonproduction costs specific to the segment have been held under control. In the case of variable costs, a determination as to the allowable or budgeted use of the variable cost is made in view of the actual sales volume. For example, in Table 8.4 the actual product-customer sales mix would allow 91,000 ton-miles of transportation and 1850 invoice equivalents of paperwork. The allowable use of variable costs is not that included in the original budget but rather reflects allowable use in view of the actual sales volume, mix, and price. Revenue-related variable costs are computed on the basis of actual revenue. Table 8.4 indicates that the district-contribution margin suffered by $3,821 due to a net unfavorable use of nonproduction variable-cost elements. The difference between the actual and budgeted use of these costs is based on only their standard costs which is the cost used for planning by the segment. Finally, the actual versus budgeted level of specific fixed costs is compared. Since there is no behavior of fixed costs with respect to volume, the benchmark used is the original budgeted expenditure.

The last component of variance analysis is an attempt to again measure promotional productivity. Table 8.5 contains an incremental analysis of district sales performance relative to incremental fixed promotional expenditures. The analysis is based on a comparison of

TABLE 8.5 ANALYSIS OF PROMOTIONAL PRODUCTIVITY

	Actual, Current	Budget Current		Actual Last Period	
		Amount	Change	Amount	Change
District contribution margin	$308,900	$338,000	$-29,100	$290,400	$18,500
Specific promotional costs	108,000	115,000	- 7,000	103,000	5,000
Incremental indicator (change in margin ÷ change in promotional costs)			4.2		3.7

actual performance to both the budget and the performance of the previous period. The analysis indicates that each dollar of promotional effort over that of the previous year produced $3.70 of contribution margin (net of all variable costs). It is also suggested that each dollar of expenditure budgeted but not spent may have lost $4.20 in contribution margin. The implied cause-effect relationship is of course heavily influenced by unquantified intervening variables such as competitors' actions, the state of the economy, the weather, and others. The indicator does, however, provide some aid in attaining the optimal level of promotional expenditure.

CHAPTER 9
Strategic
AND
Tactical
Implementation

The implementation of the principles, methods, and techniques set forth in the contribution approach requires management at all levels to possess the requisite knowledge and skill plus a favorable attitude and commitment. A key attitudinal consideration is the willingness to share cost/revenue/profit information at all levels, even to the salesman in the territory. Given these qualifications, the contribution approach is accomplished in the following ways.

First, *management by exception*, which enables attention to be focused on such matters as: the eroding profit contributions of a product, the increasing costliness of service in a market segment, the disappointing performance of a salesman, the growing need for change in distribution channels. Inasmuch as the needed information is available in real time such trouble can be nipped in the bud. This is especially critical in marketing where rapid changes and fickle customers are facts of life.

Second, *management by objectives or results* is more readily implemented. For each functional or segmental center, costs and/or revenue targets can be established and performance can be measured by the extent to which they are achieved. Thus, effective performance can be defined as:

$$AC \geq EC$$

where *AC* is actual contribution and *EC* is expected contribution. In the case of functional centers to which revenues are not attached, actual costs can be compared to projected costs. Cost variances can be interpreted in terms of standard costs when these are established.

Third, managers can more easily avoid *suboptimization*. Each center and segment manager knows that his performance will be assessed solely in terms of costs and revenues that are *attachable*. He will not be enburdened with arbitrary overhead nor with allocations beyond his control. Further, his compensation will reflect the results he achieves relative to those expected of him.

In an earlier chapter we noted the antipathies that can exist between marketing and finance. Given a commitment at the top to the principles, methods, and techniques as set forth, what are the implied responsibilities for those heading these functions?

RESPONSIBILITIES OF THE FINANCIAL EXECUTIVE

The first and primary responsibility of the financial executive is to evaluate alternative uses of money. Marketing represents one of the claimants on the uses of funds and it is the role of the financial executive to weigh the requirements of marketing against the demands of other departments and units in the corporation. In a very real sense, the financial executive represents a balance wheel in the corporation in the competition for funds.

Marketing management proposals are likely to be optimistic. A bullish attitude is almost universal among those responsible for sales. To fulfill his responsibility, the financial executive has to critically review each request for funds and compare it to alternative uses of funds in other parts of the company. Areas of conflict are minimized to the extent to which requests are supported with facts and figures. A prime use of the ideas set forth in these chapters is to facilitate such documentation for marketing management. On-line, real-time, actual data are a key antidote for subjective and capricious decision-making.

A second responsibility of the financial executive is to maintain the levels of liquidity required at different points in time by different segments of the corporation. He must insure that the company does not outrun its financial resources. He must keep the firm in healthy fiscal shape so that it may compete favorably for needed funds. His understanding of the short-term and longer term financial requirements of different marketing segments can be greatly facilitated by the specificity and accuracy of marketing performance and forecast data. The great danger in using aggregates is that they obscure varying levels of segment performance.

A third responsibility of the financial executive is to develop a financial awareness and sophistication starting at the top but extending to all management levels. The concepts and methods that we have proposed assumes accounting literacy throughout the organization!

A fourth responsibility of the financial executive is to insure that the financial information needed for marketing ties in with the total *management information system* of the company. Unless such congruity of data exists company-wide, it will be almost impossible to achieve cost/revenue/profit analysis. As an example, the coding of revenues and expenses must be congruent with the coding of purchasng and production costs, particularly as goods and services flow through the various functions into the market segments.

RESPONSIBILITIES OF THE MARKETING EXECUTIVE

A key responsibility of the marketing executive is to identify potentially profitable opportunities, combinations of new products, new markets, new channels. Application of the methods and techniques described here facilitates such evaluation and provides a basis for documenting any related recommendations.

Related to the above is responsibility for mobilizing the necessary resources to capitalize on such opportunities. Invariably this involves a request for funds and hence an interface with financial management. This puts a premium on sound budgeting. Two considerations are at issue in every proposal: *extent of potential contribution* and *timetable for realization*.

In fulfilling these two interrelated responsibilities the marketing executive must frequently depend on data that are not as "hard" as those associated with other corporate functions—for example, consider promotional cost projections for opening a new market versus costs involved in purchasing new production equipment. Thus he must make his decisions and recommendations with some degree of uncertainty. As corporate management, including finance, reviews such proposals an almost universal criterion will be applied: likelihood of success. The marketing executive must steer precariously between playing it too safe and taking undue risks.

This in turn points up a third responsibility, that of leader-trainer. It is his task to insure sufficient marketing sophistication in other functions of the organization—for example, finance, production, purchasing, research and development, so that his proposals will be understood. Within the marketing department he must insure understanding and use of contribution analysis. While finance and accounting can provide considerable expertise, the experience of many firms points up the need for the marketing executive to assume responsibility for an understanding and implementation of contribution analysis. This has given rise in many organizations to a staff specialist under the marketing executive who is designated marketing controller or similar title.

Unlike other functions, those involved in marketing, especially the sales force, are often scattered geographically. Hence, a fourth responsibility of the marketing executive is to keep communications open—upward, downward, and across—undistorted and undelayed. A well-conceived modular data base and a resultant marketing information system, as described earlier, assist in accomplishing this.

MANAGING THE MARKETING ORGANIZATION

While marketing plans and strategies are conceived in the executive suite they must be implemented throughout the marketing organization. Two points that were made in earlier sections pertain to this: First, short-term forecasting for the most part is made "bottom up." Second, function and segment managers are responsible for only those costs and revenues that are attachable. However, we also noted that a host of uncontrollable and partly controllable factors can influence marketing performance. Hence, those in lower echelons of the marketing organization must function as marketing tacticians adjusting to the unforeseen and unexpected. That is why we have espoused *flexible budgeting* and propose *decentralization* of plans, decisions, and actions as close to the market place as possible. This is especially necessary in the case of the field sales force and within the distribution network of the firm. On the negative side, nothing is likely to impair use of contribution centering more than failure on the part of headquarters marketing management to delegate. This does not mean abnegating ultimate responsibility but rather allowing for tactical adjustments by subordinates as needs arise.

EMERGING DEVELOPMENTS IN MARKETING PROFIT ANALYSIS

There are at least six emerging developments in the field of marketing profit analysis. The first development is the emergence of two new titles—Physical Distribution Financial Controller and Marketing Financial Controller. The Physical Distribution Controller is a functional analyst. The Marketing Controller is a segmental analyst. Both should be profit-oriented. Those in these two slots may well be the men most crucial to the well-being of the business in the next few years.

A second development is the need for new analytical tools to improve the marginal contributions of segments. For example, new market research tools are required for forecasting intermediate and long-term market potentials as well as short-term segments. New tools also need to be developed for relating segmental cost inputs to outputs.

A third emergence is an improvement in both segmental and functional planning and control. The improvements in segment planning will be a package of forecasting, programming, budgeting, and cost/revenue variance control. Since the segment is basically an aggregation of functions being performed, any improvement in segmental planning should facilitate physical distribution planning and control. The closer coordination between physical distribution and marketing will probably come about through the two new controllers.

A fourth development is that the modular data base will provide the information necessary for closer coordination of total competitive effort. Data can be provided on a real-time basis to determine contribution of segments, physical needs of the segment, and other data necessary for improved plans and programs.

A fifth development is the administration of the marketing information system. Since the purpose of the MIS is to furnish data on a timely basis to all sectors of the company, effective administration is important. As we noted, many companies set up the MIS independent of all existing functional and segmental divisions. Others integrate it with one or more of the principal functional users. Wherever the MIS is placed, it is clear that the administrator must be responsible for:

1. Assuring that the necessary data are available for decision-making.
2. Minimizing data errors in the system. This may necessitate an error-checking routine to handle coding errors before data are entered into the data base.
3. Furnishing clean data reports to users.
4. Checking with users to see that all data, particularly economic data, are as timely as possible.
5. Checking to see that there are limitations to expansion of the base for capricious purposes.

The title MIS Administrator seems to be evolving to meet these responsibilities. Great care needs to be exercised in the choice of this individual. He must have enough data system knowledge to select proper computer hardware and software. Yet he must also have enough functional knowledge to understand and interpret the needs of the users. This cannot be allowed to become a conflict between computer specialists and system users such as sometimes is the case. The MIS Administrator must work with system users to help them articulate their needs. He must work with the system technicians to attain performance of the system.

Sixth, new financial tools need to be developed for evaluation of segmental performance. When we abandon the net-income approach, something needs to be developed to supplant this traditional tool. It is suggested that the segment be directly charged for the cost of capital employed by that segment. Perhaps a target return on segment investment could be related to segment potential as a basis for planning customer- and product-service mixes. At any rate there are considerable opportunities for developing new financial tools. We need to develop the capability of modeling time-dependent simulations that will be useful for components and total systems planning and control.

ADDENDUM: OTHER FINANCIAL CONSIDERATIONS

In addition to the costs and revenues associated with the pretransactional, transactional, and posttransactional phases of marketing, there are three additional factors that influence directly the ultimate profitability of the firm's marketing effort. Each one has received detailed treatment by others and hence we do not propose to discuss any of them in detail. These are: *pricing, inventory evaluation,* and *compensation.*

Pricing

The plans, decisions, and actions associated with pricing are dependent upon many considerations beyond the strictly financial. For products of a commodity type the *economics* of supply and demand may be governing.[1] In virtually all cases *competitive* pricing must be considered. With many consumer goods *psychological* factors come into play. Perhaps, the most fundamental influence is the market member's assessment of *value*. In all sectors of our competitive economy the customer makes the final decision. He must see

$$V \geq P$$

[1] See Kristian S. Palda, *Pricing Decisions and Marketing Policy* (Englewood Cliffs, N.J.: Prentice-Hall, 1971).

where V (value) is equal to or greater than P (price), or he will buy the competitor's offering or not buy at all.

As to the *financial* aspect

$$P \geq C_T$$

where P (price) equals or exceeds C_T (total costs). There are a number of considerations beyond this general statement. First, for many products there are gradations of unit cost depending on the number produced and marketed. Second, there is likely to be a spread of unit-contribution across the product line. In the extreme case certain products may be offered despite the lack of contribution. Sometimes this is unwarranted and illustrates the "delusion of the full line." Third, products vary in their life expectancy and thus it is important to forecast this and to incorporate it into the final price structure. Fourth, in multidivisional companies transfer prices should meet the same criteria as those quoted to external customers. The internal purchaser in turn should have the option of "best buy" even if that means looking outside for sources.

Inventory Evaluation

Often inventories represent a major part of a firm's assets. This is especially true of various kinds of resellers. However, any firm, even if inventories do not represent a significant part of its total assets, should manage evaluation of inventories in the most realistic fashion.[2] Generally speaking three methods are used for this purpose. LIFO (last in, first out), FIFO (first in, first out), and Weighted Average.

LIFO

This method matches the cost of the latest purchases with sales. The earliest purchase prices are used to value the ending inventory. In periods of rising prices this approach produces the highest cost of goods sold and thus the lowest income. Many accountants feel that LIFO is an approximation of replacement cost and produces the most rational calculation of the profit on a sale.

FIFO

This method charges the earliest units purchased to the cost of goods sold, and the latest purchases comprise the ending inventory. FIFO

[2] See Douglas M. Lambert, *The Development of an Inventory Costing Methodology: A Study of Costs Associated with Holding Inventory* (Chicago: National Council for Physical Distribution Management, 1976).

results in a lower cost of goods sold and higher profits in periods of rising prices.

Weighted Average

Under this method the weighted-average cost of all units available during the period is applied to units sold and to units in the ending inventory. This approach may seem fair, but it results in obsolete costs assigned to both sales and inventory.

In summary, it could be said that LIFO favors the income statement since the most current costs are charged to sales, that FIFO favors the balance sheet by including the most current costs in the inventory, and that Weighted Average is neutral.

Compensation

The marketing department is necessarily *labor-intensive*—that is, many of the costs involved represent payments to personnel. In the case of all employees, other than clerical, compensation is complex and is likely to have four ingredients: salary, fringe benefits, expenses, and incentives. The incentive ingredient should be tied as directly as possible to contribution objectives which have been set in advance. Further, as a necessary control step, management should specify objectives to be met in all job duty areas, and successful achievement of these is a prerequisite to incentive compensation.[4] For example, a territory salesman may have quotas to meet, by category of account, and by product or product groups. As another example, a product manager may have objectives set in terms of quarterly demand by market segments.

[3] W. J. E. Crissy, "Salesmen—Motivating and Compensating," *Marketing Handbook*, A. W. Frey, Ed. (New York: Ronald Press, 1965), Section 12.

APPENDIX A
Coding
FOR
On-Line
AND
Off-Line Parts
OF THE
Company Data System

A fast-food chain has retail stores which are off-line, and provision must be made to incorporate them into the company data system. Stores utilize "computer cash registers" in which given types of sandwiches are provided on the buttons, together with product price information. Table A.1 shows the coding format.

As an illustration of the use of this code, assume that a hot sandwich (product code 01) is purchased from store 10, district 5, region 1, division 1. The cash register would record the following on a duplicate tape (one for the store manager's records, and one for remittance on a daily basis to the district office):

$$110510010089$$

TABLE A.1   CODING FORMAT

Position: 1 2 3 4 5 6 7 8 9 10 11 12	Position	Description	Available Digit Code Nos.
Digit: x x x x x x x x x x x	1	Division	1 to 3
	2	Region	1 to 9
	3,4	District	01 to 99
	5,6	Store	01 to 99
	7,8	Product	01 to 99
	9,10		
	11,12	Price	0001 to 99.00
	(continued)		(decimal-right-justified)

When the duplicate tape is forwarded to the district office, it is then transformed into machine-readable form for introduction into the firm's computerized data base.

Expenses, on the other hand, are handled in a somewhat different manner, given the absence of on-line capabilities in the stores. As expense transactions occur, relevant information is entered on coded forms of which one copy is kept for store records and the other is forwarded to the district office for entry into the data base.[1] Table A.2 shows a coding format utilized at the store level for expenses.

As an example of an expense transaction, if store 10, division 1, region 1, district 5 purchased 3000 super-sized hamburger patties for $1,500, it would be coded as:

$$110510501010000150003000$$

The final step to entering all information from the store segment into the data base for the company comes about at the district level. The revenue tapes are processed into machine-readable form and so is the collection of expense coding report forms forwarded to the district

[1] Before the item is entered into the data base from the base documents, an error-checking routine needs to be developed to insure the integrity of the data base. For example, a figure 1 can be read as a 7, or a 7 as a 1. These kinds of routine checks need to be checked for errors of coding before they become a part of the modular data base. It becomes extremely difficult to trace these back once the error has been committed. Therefore, one of the most obvious duties of a data-base administrator is to insure the integrity of the data base.

TABLE A.2   CODING FORMAT AT STORE LEVEL

Position:	1 2 3 4 5 6 7 8 9 10 11 12 13 14 15 16 17 18 19 20 21 22 23 24 25
Digit:	x x x x x x x x x x x x x x x x x x x x x x x x x

Position	Description	Available Digit Code Nos.
1	Division	1 to 3
2	Region	1 to 9
3,4	District	01 to 99
5,6	Store	01 to 99
7,8,9	Account no.	400 to 99
10,11	Subaccount or product nos. where applicable	01 to 99
12–19	Amount	00000001 to 999999.99 (actually decimal effect is machine-right-justified)
20–25	Quantity purchased	00001 to 999999

office. Both chains of information flows are processed through on-line terminals at the district office where they are sorted and filed by the computer in the final coded form. A suggested final coded form resembles that shown in Table A.3.

The numbers available for the digit codes are the same as those explained in the preceding examples with the exception of the transaction codes. This code number is either 0 or 1, 0 indicating an expense transaction and 1 indicating a revenue or sales transaction. The primary purpose of this transaction code would be to facilitate the aggregation of revenues and expenses at succeedingly high levels throughout the organization.

A suggested alternative form for coding that is an improvement on the two-digit requirement for some of the items in the code is the following alternative:

$$111111111222222 \ldots 77778$$
$$12345678901234567890123456 \ldots 67890$$

This field can easily go into the 80 columns provided for in the standard data card format used in many computer systems. It has the distinct advantage of conserving space laterally and not requiring the double digits used in the illustration above.

TABLE A.3   SUGGESTED FINAL CODED FORM

| Description: | Division | Region | District | Store | Trans-action Code | Acct. No. | Subacct. No. | $ Amt. | Quantities |
| Position: Digit | 1 | 1 | 3,4 | 5,6 | 7 | 8,9,10 | 11,12 | 13–20 | 21–26 |

APPENDIX B
Important
External Codes

The following is a brief description of some of the more important external codes. the codes that will be described include the Standard Industrial Classification Code, the Standard Internal Trade Classification Code, Transportation Commodity Classification Code, and Schedules A and B of the Standard Classifications of U.S. Domestic and Foreign Commodities.[1]

The Standard Industrial Classification Code is a five-digit code reflecting the principal activity of a given company's manufacturing operations. Each major group is indicated by a two-digit code and each subgroup under the major group by succeeding digits. The SIC is a commonly used coding for all domestic activities and in some other countries in the world. In the United States it is under the supervision of the U.S. Bureau of the Census.

As an example of the use of SIC codes to classify customers into target markets, consider the case of a storage battery manufacturer in Figure B.1. The company sells batteries to motor vehicle, aircraft, and locomotive manufacturers who use them as components of their own products. Also they sell them to electrical apparatus and equipment distributors, who provide batteries or supplies to various manufacturers using battery-operated equipment. Finally, through automotive parts and

[1] Great opportunities exist for combining internal analysis with external data provided by the input-output tables prepared by the U.S. Department of Commerce and by various industries. Much work has been done by industry groups and by some of the larger companies in which the cell-by-cell analysis of the customer-product mix is tied in with input-output analysis.

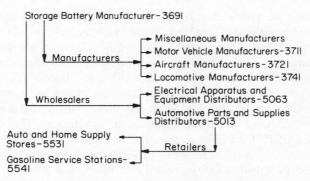

Figure B.1.   Use of SIC codes.

supplies distributors, they reach auto and some supply stores and gasoline service stations where the batteries are sold to the consumer market as replacement parts. Notice that each type of customer is described by that four-digit SIC code which indicates the company's classification as manufacturer, wholesaler, or retailer and the product class of its primary product.

The Standard International Trade Code is a code based on 625 subgroups of products identified by code numbers of four digits. The basic four-digit groups are further subdivided to distinguish commodities of statistical importance. The resulting SITC is a five-digit code on an item level. It was developed for products in international trade by the United Nations to coincide with the nomenclature referred to as BTN (Brussels Trade Nomenclature).

The Transportation Commodity Classification Code is a five-digit code very similar to the SIC code and it is used for all series in the U.S. Census of Transportation. The TCC is becoming widely accepted in the transportation field in general. Administrative agencies of the Federal government as well as many carriers have adopted the code for internal and external use. The U.S. Census of Transportation is broken down into several surveys that indicate flow characteristics of commodities in the geographic areas of the United States. Flows of goods are indicated by three general geographic breakdowns: (1) from states within geographic divisions, (2) geographic division to geographic division, and (3) major industrial centers to major industrial centers.

Schedules A and B of the Standard Classification of Domestic and Foreign Commodities is a code system developed to permit the comparison of U.S. import and export statistics with foreign trade statistics reported by other countries in terms of the Standard International Trade

Classification. Schedule A is a code for U.S. imports and Schedule B is a code for U.S. exports. The code numbers may have as many as seven digits and are much more specific than the SITC and in some cases more specific than the SIC. The first, second, and third digits are exactly comparable to the Standard International Trade Classification.

In order to trace the use of these various codes, a commodity has been selected for location in each of these various groupings. The commodity selected is office duplicating machines. The SIC group number is 35791; Table B.1 represents the flows of this product from Chicago to various market areas in the eastern corridor.

This type of information is readily available for all SIC categories making it relatively easy to trace various product flows from one market area to another. A broader measure of product flow may be obtained from the Census of Business which gives product flows which originate from various geographic areas such as northeast, south-central, and so forth. The Census of Transportation also gives the flow of different SIC categories from market areas in terms of the means of transportation and distance of shipment.

While there is no real trouble in measuring product flows with various SICs domestically, there is some difficulty in tracing a particular SIC category through international markets. This problem is a result of the many different code numbers for office duplicating machines (714.9110–714.9170). The SIC code lumps all types of these machines into one code number—35791 (which also includes mailing machines and check writing machines). The SITC code uses 714.2 to represent calculators, accounting, and other office machines. The broad category of "statistical machines" is 714.3. This code is based upon the *Yearbook of International Trade Statistics,* published by the United Nations.

Thus, a great deal of effort is required to cross-reference each different code, depending on the source of information used. If we wanted to trace SIC 35791 through international markets, we would first have to ensure that SIC 35791 was comparable to either the SITC or Schedule B code to be used. If the SITC included more products than were included in the SIC, we would, of course, have to adjust the SITC accordingly. But SIC 35791 is much broader than another corresponding

TABLE B.1　AN SIC CODE

	Tons Distributed to Area Destination from Chicago			
SIC	Boston	New York	Philadelphia	Baltimore
35791	212,000	2,915,000	560,000	265,000

TABLE B.2   SAMPLE CODE CROSS-CLASSIFICATION

Schedule B Code	Product	SITC Code	SIC Code
714	Office machines	71410	357
714.1	Typewriters	71420	3572
714.2002	Digital computers	71420	35731
714.2025	Elec. adding machines	71420	35741
714.9110	Duplicating machines		35791

Schedule B code. Thus, Schedule B 714.9110 through 714.9170 would have to be totaled to get a figure somewhat comparable to SIC 35791. If United Nations data were used, SITC code number 714.3 is the code corresponding to SIC 35791. But SITC 714.3 is broader than SIC 35791, and it would have to be adjusted downward. Furthermore, data was for shipments value, not tons.

The Department of Commerce has developed a cross-classification of different codes which will hopefully lead to facilitating the comparability of various codes (Table B.2).

APPENDIX C
Alternative Segmental Combinations

The various levels of management reflected throughout the organizational structure show a need for alternative segmental combinations for different types of decisions, different levels of decision-making, and different time frames. Some examples of these needs for alternative combinations are shown for a small retail chain and a small hospitality firm.

In order to illustrate that the contribution approach and a modular base are not exclusively reserved for large companies with complex computer systems, a small retail chain is shown in Table C.1. This is a small three-store chain of jewelry stores. Each of these stores is a small kiosk which sells jewelry in a shopping center in a high-traffic-density location. In Table C.1 the income and expense for the company in total are shown, and the segment-contribution margin is shown for store number 2 in Table C.2. A breakdown for one of the stores shows the product-line contributions for each of the five product lines handled in the store. This can be done for each store and then summed across store lines as desired. All of this is done simply by using the tapes off the case register and does not necessitate a complicated computer system.

Contribution in a small motel-restaurant combination is presented in Tables C.3 and C.4 to show the applicability of the concept to a small business from the hospitality industry. The net income approach for the business is shown in Table C.3; this approach shows the motel contributing more to net income than the restaurant. The contribution approach

TABLE C.1 contribution in a small retail chain

	Company Total	%	Divisions					
			Store 1	%	Store 2	%	Store 3	%
Net sales	$262,807	100	$96,085	100	$113,084	100	$53,638	100
Direct variable costs								
COGS	131,405		48,044		56,542		26,819	
Rent (var. portion)	7,234		1,926		5,308		0	
Bonuses	567		245		215		107	
Prop. tax-inv.	1,926		446		1,077		403	
Cost of cap. (inv.)	4,000		1,375		1,550		1,075	
Total variable costs	145,132	55.2	52,036	54.2	64,692	57.2	28,404	53
Segment contribution margin	117,675	44.8	44,049	45.8	48,392	42.8	25,234	47
Direct fixed costs								
Rent	17,760		5,760		6,000		6,000	
Wages (sales)	24,630		7,938		9,623		7,069	
Soc. Sec. & Unempl. Ins.	2,069		667		808		594	
Electric	665		72		408		185	
Phone	1,080		360		360		360	
Merchant assoc. dues	375		125		125		125	
Displays	540		180		180		180	
Cost of cap. (store)*	2,322		822		750		750	
Deprec. (store)†	2,322		822		750		750	
Total fixed costs	51,763	19.7	16,746	17.4	19,004	16.8	16,013	29.9
Segment controllable margin	65,912	25.1	27,303	28.4	29,388	26.0	9,221	17.1
Company fixed costs								
Wages (mgt.)	8,582							
Insurance	300							
Legal & prof.	250							
Miscellaneous	5,090							
Total company fixed costs	14,222	5.4						
Net residual income	$ 51,690	19.7						

* Cost of capital was calculated at a rate of 10%.
† Depreciation was calculated using the straight line method and assuming a ten year life of the assets.

TABLE C.2 STORE NUMBER TWO OF THE RETAIL CHAIN

	Division Total		14K Earrings		14K Pendants		14K Rings		Watches		Costume	
	Amount	%	Amount	%	Amount	%	Amount	%	Amount	%	Amount	%
	Product Lines											
Net sales	$113,084	100	$4,636	100	$3,619	100	$5,654	100	$1,696	100	$97,479	100
Direct variable costs												
Bonuses	215		0		0		215		0		0	
COGS	56,542		2,318		1,809		2,827		848		48,740	
Prop. tax-inv.	197		26		10		51		6		104	
Cost of cap. (inv.)	1,550		206		76		403		47		818	
Total variable costs	58,504	51.7	2,550	55.0	1,895	52.4	3,496	61.8	901	53.1	49,662	50.9
Segment contribution margin	54,580	48.3	2,086	45.0	1,724	47.6	2,158	38.2	795	46.9	47,817	49.1
Direct fixed costs												
Displays	180	.16	180	3.9	0		0		0		0	
Segment controllable margin	54,400	48.1	1,906	41.1	1,724	47.6	2,158	38.2	795	46.9	47,817	49.1
Division fixed costs												
Rent	$ 11,308											
Wages	9,623											
Electric	408											
Phone	360											
Merch. assoc. dues	125											
Prop. tax (store)	880											
Cost cap. (store)	750											
Deprec. (store)	750											
Soc. Sec. & Unempl. Ins.	808											
Total division fixed costs	$ 25,012	22.1										
Net segment margin	$ 29,388	26.0										

TABLE C.3   NET INCOME IN A HOSPITALITY FIRM FOR A CALENDAR YEAR

	Total		Restaurant		Motel	
Sales		$120,340		$97,364		$22,976
Cost of goods sold	$43,316	43,316	$43,316	43,316		-0-
Gross profit		$ 77,024		$54,048		$22,976
Expenses						
Sales & use tax	$ 4,682		$ 3,721		$ 961	
Payroll tax	2,739		2,452		287	
Wages	31,133		27,873		3,260	
Utilities	5,663		3,810		1,853	
Advertising*	2,983		1,893		1,090	
Ins. fees, taxes*	1,736		1,157		579	
Depreciation	7,458		3,494		3,964	
Supplies*	2,077		1,661		416	
Property tax	1,462		795		667	
Maintenance*	168		134		34	
Net income operations	60,101	$ 16,923	46,990	$ 7,058	13,111	$ 9,865
Other expenses						
Interest exp.		14,350				
Net profit		$ 2,573				

* Common costs are allocated by percentage of sales—80% restaurant and 20% motel.

TABLE C.4   CONTRIBUTION IN A HOSPITALITY FIRM FOR A CALENDAR
YEAR

| | Segments | | |
	Restaurant	Motel	Total
Sales	$97,364	$22,976	$120,340
Less variable costs			
COGS	43,316	—	43,316
Sales and use tax	3,721	961	4,682
Payroll taxes	2,452	287	2,739
Wages	27,873	3,260	31,133
Utilities	3,810	1,853	5,663
Total variable costs	$81,172	$ 6,361	$87,533
Segment contribution margin	$16,192	$16,615	$32,807
Less programmed short-run variable costs			
Advertising	—	617	617
Insurance	—	290	290
Depreciation (straight line)	3,494	3,964	7,458
Property tax	795	667	1,462
Cost of capital inventory of $1500 10%	150	—	150
Total programmed costs	$ 4,439	$ 5,538	$ 9,977
Segment controllable margin	$11,753	$11,077	$22,830
Less Long-run cost specific to segment			
cost of capital at replacement			
Motel bldg. & equipment $86,000 @ 10%		8,600	8,600
Restaurant bldg. & equipment $52,000 @ 10%	5,200		5,200
Net segment margin	$ 6,553	$ 2,477	$ 9,030
Business common costs			
Supplies not separable			$ 2,077
Insurance, fees, taxes			1,447
Maintenance			168
Advertising			2,365
Cost of capital $4,000 @ 10%			400
Total common costs			$ 6,457
Net residual income			$ 2,573

is used in Table C.4, and here the restaurant makes a greater contribution than does the motel. The contribution approach used here also shows cost of capital as segment expense in both programmed and long-run cost categories. More useful planning is obtainable with the contribution by market segment.

APPENDIX D

CHANGES IN

Market
Trading Areas

This appendix is included to show how changes occur in market trading areas. Every physical location—whether it be a city, region, plant, warehouse, or retail store—has a geographic area within which the products or services of the given location are sold. This is the market trading area. It is an important form of market segmentation.

The market trading area goes through a life cycle as do other market segments. Two aspects of changes in trading areas are discussed: first, an example of a trading area in Lansing, Michigan for the years 1969 to 1972; and, second, customers' temporal perceptions as related to trading area limits.

TRADING AREA CHANGE IN LANSING, MICHIGAN[1]

In a marketing context much effort has been expended in locating the geographic trading area of an established retail store or, conversely, to determine the proper location of a proposed retail facility to obtain maximum geographic drawing power. In these studies consideration is given to the relative highway access of the store, population density,

[1] This material is taken from *A Case Study of Retail Competition, Metropolitan Lansing, Michigan, 1969–1972* (unpublished study by Paul E. Smith, Professor Emeritus of Marketing, Graduate School of Business, Michigan State University, 1975).

157

TABLE D.1 PROPORTION OF TRADE BY DISTANCE
FROM CITY CENTER FOR LANSING

	Cumulative Percent of Total				
	0–1 Mile	0–2 Miles	0–3 Miles	0–4 Miles	Over 4 Miles
April 1969	17	47	68	87	100
April 1970	18	50	74	89	100
April 1972	32	61	78	83	100

demographic customer data, and competitive store locations. It is this last factor that will be illustrated here.

The map of major shopping centers in the Lansing area is shown in Figure D.1. The major centers covered in the study were: (1) Lansing central business district, (2) East Lansing central business district, (3) Frandor Mall, constructed in 1954, (4) Lansing Mall, constructed in 1969, and (5) Meridian Mall: constructed in 1969.

The effect of the opening of the three malls on the trading areas of the Lansing and East Lansing central business districts was as follows:

1. The Lansing central business district shrank considerably to the area encompassed by the dashed line (Table D.1). Thus, the Lansing central business district was narrowed geographically between 1969 and 1972. Higher percentages of trade were coming from areas closer to the central business district.

2. The East Lansing central business district (the dashed-dot line) was hit even harder by the opening of the malls (Table D.2). Between 1969 and 1970 the strictly neighborhood trade of zero to one mile had increased from 39 to 65 percent of total.

TABLE D.2 PROPORTION OF TRADE BY DISTANCE
FROM CITY CENTER FOR EAST LANSING

	Cumulative Percent of Total				
	0–1 Mile	0–2 Miles	0–3 Miles	0–4 Miles	Over 4 Miles
April 1969	39	77	88	96	100
April 1970	47	63	72	81	100
June 1971	65	81	94	100	100

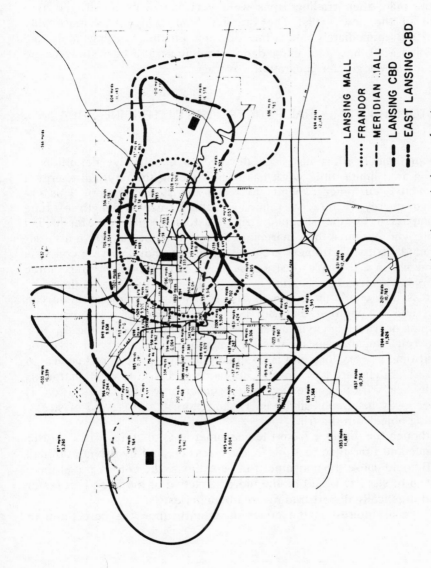

Figure D.1. 1970 census map comparing size and shape of patronage profiles of five shopping centers.

LANSING MALL
FRANDOR
MERIDIAN MALL
LANSING CBD
EAST LANSING CBD

159

Other changes of course have occurred over time. Although the neighborhood shopping centers and free-standing stores are not shown on the map, their trading areas were very narrowly constricted as a result of the new malls. The Frandor Mall, which was reasonably moribund immediately after the opening of the Lansing Mall and Meridian Mall, has since expanded its trading area; a later study would probably show greater geographic coverage.

CUSTOMERS' TEMPORAL PERCEPTIONS OF TRADING-AREA LIMITS

Although much effort has been devoted to quantitative definition of trading area limits, little work has been done on the physical energy a prospective customer expends to reach the store location. This expended energy is directly related to the perceived length of time encompassed by the shopping trip. Customers are not Marshallian people who optimize their marginal costs of disability to arrive at least-cost modal trips. Customers are individuals who have varying concepts of time which will vary with stress, activity, and motivation. These three factors have special application to marketing- and trading-area limits.

Stress is a condition in which distortions of temporal duration can result and a condition that can be prevalent for the customer in a shopping or traveling environment. A person who perceives the trip to a given retail location as a stressful situation is going to perceive the transit time as very long and is less likely to shop there. For instance in Figure D.2 there are two store locations, A and C, a town B characterized by heavy traffic congestion, and a consumer located at C. Store C is farther away geographically from D than store C but is void of stress-creating objects on the trip.

Although the distance from the consumer at C to store A is a shorter distance and time than to store C, the stress created by driving through city B could cause the consumer to overestimate the D-to-A travel time. The trip to store C would be the more attractive of the two. This factor would drastically distort trading-area boundaries.

Of similar interest is the effect of activity upon the perception of

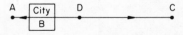

Figure D.2.   An example of stress.

duration. Three observations seem pertinent:

1. The degree of overestimation of time duration increases as the degree of difficulty increases. If concentration can be induced as a requirement to task performance, the shorter seems the duration of time.
2. Fatigue time is nearly always overestimated, making it an extremely unattractive activity.
3. Active time intervals are perceived as shorter than inactive intervals.

The degree to which the temporal interval is perceived to be pleasant or unpleasant determines the amount of motivation an individual has to complete that interval. Motivation is difficult to measure but it has marketing implications in that marketers must create "pleasant" product images in order to attract the more distant customers and expand the geographic limits of the trading area.

The measurement application of these temporal perceptions to the life cycle of a trading area is difficult. Nevertheless the concepts need to be incorporated in both short-run and long-run programming. The ideal time to incorporate them is when the site is selected. All too often a site is selected and then turned over to the merchandising departments to make a profit. Improperly conceived perceptions of stress, activity, and motivation may lead in later stages of the cycle to nothing but ulcers and heart attacks for merchandise managers.

Since trading area life cycles change in much the same way as product life cycles, an understanding of this can help to develop segments that contribute to profit. Therefore it is desirable to have in the data base the alternative of classifying revenue and expense by component parts of the trading area as well as by other types of market segments.

AUTHOR INDEX

SUBJECT INDEX